HIDDEN MIRACLES OF THE BIBLE

Secret Wisdom Within the Word

by Brent S. Furrow

DEFIANCE PRESS
& PUBLISHING

Hidden Miracles of the Bible: Secret Wisdom Within the Word

DEFIANCE PRESS
& PUBLISHING

ISBN-13: 978-1-959677-08-6 (Paperback)
ISBN-13: 978-1-959677-07-9 (eBook)

Published by Defiance Press and Publishing, LLC

Bulk orders of this book may be obtained by contacting Defiance Press and Publishing, LLC. www.defiancepress.com.

Public Relations Dept. – Defiance Press & Publishing, LLC
281-581-9300
pr@defiancepress.com

Defiance Press & Publishing, LLC
281-581-9300
info@defiancepress.com

TABLE OF CONTENTS

INTRODUCTION

"I remember the days of old; I meditate on all that you have done; I ponder the work of your hands." | Psalm 143:5

Who isn't captivated by a miracle? While I think most people would agree that we would all love to experience one of God's epic miracles in our lives, the definition of the word has lost much of its luster today in our modern world. We often use phrases like "It's a miracle that I made it into work today," or "It's a miracle it didn't rain on my outdoor barbeque this weekend." While those moments might be lucky or fortuitous, they're hardly miraculous.

Theologian Wayne Grudem defines miracles as "a less common kind of God's activity in which he arouses people's awe and wonder and bears witness to himself. He justifies this definition by awe, or amazement in such a way that God shows himself as true." Baker's Dictionary of Theology defines a miracle as "an event in the external world brought about by the immediate agency or the simple volition of God." It goes on to add that a miracle occurs to show that the power behind it is not limited to the laws of matter or the mind, and it interrupts fixed natural scientific laws. Thus, the fact that you didn't hit the snooze button four times this morning and weren't late to work today clearly cannot be considered supernatural. While your morning alarm might have interrupted your beauty rest, it was hardly a divine interruption of fixed natural laws.

It's important to consider the truth that a miracle that interferes with natural law does not mean that a natural law must be broken. If a car stalls on the train tracks at a desolate railroad crossing and a bus load of high school football players just so happen to be behind it, and the players all pile out to push the car off the rails just before a freight train comes barreling through, no natural law was broken. However, God did miraculously provide the means for a disaster to be avoided.

In the book *The Rescue*, which describes the crash of a plane in the Bering Sea, Dave Anderson recounts how the pilot of his missionary plane in Alaska that lost power just so happened to direct their plane to a safe landing in the ocean, where everyone survived the impact. The plane just so happened to be carrying seventeen empty gas cans that could be used for buoyancy as flotation devices for the passengers. They also just so happened to be spotted in the water by a passing commuter plane that just so happened to be fortuitously running an hour late that day. Two helicopters, fully fueled and with pilots on duty, just so happened to be in that vicinity—in one of the most remote parts of the world. And everybody on that missionary flight just so happened to survive not only a plane crash and drowning but hypothermia, too. Now *that's* one heck of a miracle.

It's widely debated how many Old Testament and New Testament miracles are listed in the Bible, and a quick internet search will yield all sorts of thoughts and opinions. Many miracles are extraordinary and clearly evidenced, such as the Great Flood, the Parting of the Red Sea, or Jesus' act of raising Lazarus from the dead. But as you read the Bible closer, you'll discover lots of miracles that are a little more hidden, a bit more latent. They're miracles within miracles—words within the word that are slightly more concealed. Some are speculative, and you'll have to read between the lines to discover the possibility of them. For others, they're an aligning of events or supernatural language in different parts of the Bible that are so interconnected, so astonishing and co-incidental, that the only explanation is that God miraculously wove them together so we could bear witness to His divinity.

A lifelong Christian, I grew up and was baptized and confirmed as a Lutheran. I regularly attended church during my childhood and was involved in my youth group when I was younger. I participated in Bible studies in college and throughout my young adult life, but it wasn't until I began to do more solo Bible study and independently build a greater biblical understanding that I began to discover some of these less apparent miracles in the Bible, and the deep wisdom in which they're shrouded.

As an airline captain for a charter airline, I have moments of intense workloads where I'm extremely busy with the great respon-sibility to safely and efficiently transport passengers to their next destination. Some days, I'm tasked to complete five or six flights and barely have time to shower, sleep, and grab some food on the run. But oftentimes I have lots of downtime. Moments where I'm sitting in a business jet terminal late at night waiting for a sports team's charter buses to return to the airport after an away game so we can fly to the next city. Other days, I might be in a hotel in some foreign locale for a day or two with no transportation to go out and do anything, inclement weather, or security that's less than ideal for taking a walk or any outdoor recreation. In these periods of downtime, I often turn to Bible study, hungry for the Word. In these moments, God has revealed secrets of the Bible to me that I never before recognized.

Isaiah 43:19 says, "See, I am doing a new thing! Now it springs up; do you not perceive it? I am making a way in the wilderness and streams in the wasteland." God was actively working in the lives of the Israelites in the Old Testament. He was active in the lives of the New Testament disciples and early Christian community, growing them, molding them, and transforming them. He is always refining things in this world, defining and shaping the facets of your life and my life, even today. Hebrews 4:12 says, "The word of God is alive and active." Unlike a dusty decades-old textbook up on a shelf, frozen in time, the Bible is living and breathing, and there are always new insights to discover, new revelations to find.

Come along with me on this journey to discover some of the hidden secrets of the Bible, lesser known divine moments authored by God, and the wisdom he imparts that you may have never before noticed. I am eager to share with you what's been revealed to me through my studies. While this is in no way a complete list, as there are certainly numerous other hidden miracles, I hope and pray that these examples provide encouragement for you to keep your eyes open when reading your Bible and studying His word to discover some hidden divinity yourself.

His word says, "On the glorious splendor of your majesty, and on your wondrous works, I will meditate," (Psalm 145:5) and "Make me understand the way of your precepts, and I will meditate on your wondrous works" (Psalm 119:27). May our Lord and

Savior lead you and guide you to grow closer to Him as you deepen your meditation and ponder His heavenly works.

CHAPTER 1: MIRACLE OF JOSHUA AND THE JORDAN RIVER

.୭ල ୨ର.

*"When you pass through the waters, I will be
with you; and when you pass through the rivers,
they will not sweep over you."* | Isaiah 43:2

Several summers ago, I headed out west to visit a second cousin living in Saint Maries, Idaho. He invited me to camp with him and try my hand at fly-fishing in the Coeur d'Alene National Forest way up in the Idaho panhandle. I'm a sucker for trying new things, especially if they spark the inner pioneer cowboy spirit in me. John Eldredge said it best: "Deep in his heart, every man longs for a battle to fight, an adventure to live," and this was my chance to feed my inner nature lover. Eating homemade pancakes over the campfire with wild huckleberries we picked just that morning was thrilling. Looking up at a million stars in the heavens, like Abraham did in Genesis 15:5, and seeing the Milky Way each night brought out a sense of awe and wonder in me that I could have never experienced amid light pollution back home in St. Louis. Fly-fishing was a lot of fun, although I think I only caught a couple of trout. It would take several more lessons before I could ever possess skills worthy of *A River Runs Through It*.

New to this sport, I learned that you have to wear special felt-bottom boots that help you walk on the slippery moss-covered rocks as you wade out into the river. They give you traction as the swift current pushes against your legs and tries to take you downstream to the Pacific Ocean, or wherever it eventually ends up on the other side of the Continental Divide. Wading out into ankle-deep water is a cinch. Venturing further into knee-deep water is a challenge, but doable. Any deeper than that, though, and I'm like a baby giraffe trying to walk for the first time; the current was too much for me to withstand. All at once, I came crashing down with a big splash! Wet and frustrated, we decided to call it a day and headed back to camp. Luckily for the spies described in the book of Joshua, they had no trouble crossing a surging Jordan River twice, however they did it—and they never lost their footing.

The story begins after the death of Moses. God has installed Joshua as the new leader of the Israelites as they continued their trek to the promised land. A generation forty years prior had witnessed one of the most prolific miracles of all time: the parting of the Red Sea. Now, a new generation needed reassurance that God was still with them as they prepared to conquer the city of Jericho that stood in their way. Joshua 3:14-17 says:

> So it was, when the people set out from their camp to cross over the Jordan, with the priests bearing the ark of the covenant before the people, and as those who bore the ark came to the Jordan, and the feet of the priests who bore the ark dipped in the edge of the water (for the Jordan overflows all its banks during the whole time of harvest), that the waters which came down from upstream stood still, and rose in a heap very far away at Adam, the city that *is* beside Zaretan. So the waters that went down into the Sea of the Arabah, the Salt Sea, failed,

and were cut off; and the people crossed over opposite Jericho. Then the priests who bore the ark of the covenant of the Lord stood firm on dry ground in the midst of the Jordan; and all Israel crossed over on dry ground, until all the people had crossed completely over the Jordan.

Now that's pretty darn cool, but let's remember what happened in Joshua 2 just prior to the moment when the power of the ark of the covenant held the Jordan River at bay. Joshua had sent two spies ahead of the rest of the Israelites to survey the city. They were famously kept hidden by Rahab, the prostitute who helped them with safe passage to flee the city while they evaded the King of Jericho's men trying to hunt them down. Joshua 2:23 says that the spies "crossed over" the Jordan River, and this is where we find a **hidden miracle**. The spies would have had to initially cross over the river the first time to *get* to Jericho, and then a second time *returning back* to the Israelite camp *from* Jericho. There were not one, in fact, but two miraculous crossings!

Rivers change course over time, but one consistency among all rivers is they have swift currents, invisible undertows that aren't apparent from merely looking at the surface, deep pockets, and uneven river bottoms. The Jordan River flows sixty miles from the Sea of Galilee to the Dead Sea, and over the course of those sixty miles, it drops over six hundred feet in elevation. That's a ten-foot drop every mile in length, and we know the river was above flood stage as the Bible describes it, so it was likely flowing around ten miles per hour. On top of that, all sorts of debris would have been rushing downstream with the raging current.

For comparison's sake, the midpoint of the Mississippi River in the United States from St. Louis to the Ohio River confluence drops only 1.2 feet per mile, and that is still an extremely dangerous stretch of water. Thus, the Jordan River flowing nine times that speed would have been like whitewater rapids! Such a current would be way too dangerous to swim, and in fact, an expert swimmer tried to cross the Jordan in 1854 to prove it could be done—and didn't make it.

The Bible doesn't tell us how the spies were able to cross the river, only that they "crossed over." We know there is no way they walked across, and they certainly didn't take a ferry boat or hike across a footbridge. As spies, it's likely they also had to move under the cover of darkness to avoid getting caught, and nighttime travel would have posed yet an additional challenge. Perhaps God parted the river specifically for them, like he later did for the rest of the Israelites, and the Bible just doesn't mention it. But no matter how the spies crossed the Jordan, they somehow did it twice, under absolutely miraculous circumstances.

Another important note about the **hidden miracle** of the spies crossing the Jordan is that to God, this apparently wasn't even worth specifically mentioning. Much more press is given to the spies' coordination with Rahab than to the divine methods of how God enabled the spies to cross the river, which shows that God is much more concerned with people's salvation and their hearts than bending the laws of nature to allow safe passage through a river. The river crossing to God is just . . .*meh*. There's a greater lesson in hospitality, commitment, redemption, and salvation than there is in a dramatic river crossing. Even so, the spies' journey through the Jordan is an incredible feat, however it happened.

CHAPTER 2: MIRACLE OF JONAH AND THE ROMAN CONVERSION

๛๏ ๏๛

"Where can I go to escape Your Spirit? Where can I flee from Your presence?" | Psalm 139:7

I f I could meet any Bible character other than Jesus himself, it would be Jonah. Jonah surviving for three days in the belly of the fish is incredible, but curiously, it isn't a story you'll often hear preached during a Sunday sermon. What a way to spend a long weekend, though. When Jonah woke up that morning, I bet those overnight accommodations were nowhere near the realm of his thoughts. TripAdvisor recommendation of "0" stars. The story of Jonah tends to be taught as more of a vacation Bible school lesson, which is too bad for us adults, because this story has many lessons for us as well.

What makes Jonah interesting and compelling to me is that he is rebellious and stubborn; he has his own mental battles to contend with. He has certain vulnerabilities and insecurities and is tempted to run from his problems rather than face them. He knows he should take one path, yet he hightails it in the opposite direction. But God chases after him and offers him redemption and, ultimately, love. How great it is that our God is a God of second chances.

Jonah is real. Authentic. He's like one of us. I can identify with Jonah's challenges myself, and I'm eternally thankful that God throws a lasso around me every once in a while when I start to veer off course and imparts me to straighten up and get my act together. As humans, we are given an opportunity to ask for forgiveness, correct our ways, and return to Him. Proverbs 16:9 says, "In their hearts, humans plan their course, but the Lord establishes their steps." Praise God that when we rebel or when fear sets in and we take our eyes off Jesus, He offers us diversions and course corrections. He gives us safe harbor for us to find anchorage when the seas of life get a little too rough to handle alone.

The story of Jonah hinges around a point of fear more so than a lack of ability. God saw that the ancient city of Nineveh was evil and was rebelling against him, so he commissioned Jonah to preach the good news to the people to get them to change their ways. In many ways, Nineveh parallels Sodom, another city in the Old Testament as described in Genesis 18-19 where God sent a messenger of warning. Fear washes over Jonah, as Jonah 3:3 describes the city as being so large that it literally takes "three days" to walk through. Jonah was afraid there were no righteous people left in the city, that he'd be preaching to a brick wall among enemies. Perhaps you can identify with that sort of fear—it's much easier to offer a sales pitch to a group where at least some of the people think and reason the same way you do and you at least have a couple of allies in the room, rather than a room of hostility where nobody wants to hear your message.

The lesson that Jonah was slow to realize was that Jonah needed Nineveh as much as Nineveh needed Jonah. Jonah's escape in the opposite direction was because of his lack of understanding of how many believers were actually left within Nineveh. He felt alone, isolated, and gripped by fear that he was the only righteous man in the midst of a great big city. Sure, there were many wicked people, but there were many righteous ones as well. God created all of us with the need for fellowship and community. Just like God knew that this man, feeling as though he were an outcast swimming all alone in a sea of sharks, needed to recognize that if he just looked hard enough, he would find fellow believers to cling to.

The lesson in proselytizing displayed through Jonah's fear is that while we are called to spread the gospel to others, it's also important to also have that strong community of fellow Christians. Your church family serves as your confidants and accountability partners to "build each other up," giving you strength and encouragement as you courageously step foot onto the mission field (1 Thessalonians 5:11). Jonah 4:11 says that Nineveh had over 120,000 unrighteous inhabitants, but it likely had many more who were faithful that Jonah could've first sought out for support. But he did not.

With the cards stacked against him and gripped by fear, Jonah decides he's not up for the challenge of trying to change the hearts of an entire city. So, he punches out and buys a boat ticket for Tarshish—a land about 2,500 miles in the opposite direction of Nineveh, virtually the farthest reaches of the known world at that time. In his mind, the best way to avoid a problem was to remove himself from the equation altogether.

While on the boat, Jonah falls asleep and a big storm kicks up, tossing the little boat to and fro on the waves. It parallels the story of Mark 4 when Jesus was asleep on a boat and the disciples woke him out of fear (more on that story later). These hardened, experienced Roman sailors were so terrified that they awoke Jonah and told him to pray to "his god" to calm the seas. Jonah 1: 8-16 describes the dialogue:

> So they asked him, "Tell us, who is responsible for making all this trouble for us? What kind of work do you do? Where do you come from? What is your country? From what people are you?" He answered, "I am a Hebrew and I worship the Lord, the God of heaven, who made the sea and the dry land." This terrified them and they asked, "What have you done?" (They knew he was running away from the Lord, because he had already told them so.) The sea was getting rougher and rougher. So they asked him, "What should we do to you to make the sea calm down for us?" "Pick me up and throw me into the sea," he replied, "and it will become calm. I know that it is my fault that this great storm has come upon you." Instead, the men did their best to row back to land. But they could not, for the sea grew even wilder than before. Then they cried out to the Lord, "Please, Lord, do not let us die for taking this man's life. Do not hold us accountable for killing an innocent man, for you, Lord, have done as you pleased." Then they took Jonah and threw him overboard, and the raging sea grew calm. At this the men greatly feared the Lord, and they offered a sacrifice to the Lord and made vows to him.

We find here what I think is one of the coolest hidden miracles of the entire Bible. Actually, there are a couple, and they culminate in the overarching miracle of salvation. But most importantly, we learn of the conversion of these Roman sailors, whose names have long been lost to history but are certainly known to God. The Romans and Hebrews didn't exactly get along. The multiple Roman sailors could have easily overpowered Jonah and immediately cast him overboard, but they did not. It is a miracle in its own right that the Romans initially spared Jonah's life and tried to protect him, doing their best to row the boat to shore, for Jonah's life was nothing to them. They did not have any personal connection with him; he was just a vagrant, a rambler, a rolling stone who had hitched a ride aboard their boat to get out of town. The important takeaway in their delay in casting Jonah immediately overboard is that we are called to love all people, both familial and foreign.

When Jonah insisted that the only way to calm the seas and appease God was to throw him overboard, the sailors reluctantly did so, but not without first offering a prayer up to "the Lord," a God they did not know. This is the moment where their conversion starts, and a subtle **hidden miracle** is found in the scripture of this story. The Roman sailors didn't want murder on their hands, and they knew that casting a passenger into the angry sea would almost certainly result in death by drowning for Jonah. But when Jonah persisted, they did so, and the seas instantly grew calm.

Pause there for a moment. Have you ever been out in a little pleasure boat when a summer thunderstorm kicked up and the waves quickly turned wicked? If not, think of the last movie you saw when there was a ship on the seas about to go under. Picture the rage of the waves, the fury of the wind, rain beating down, so debilitating that you can barely even stand on the deck of the boat. A pure loss of control of the situation. Then, in the story of Jonah, in that moment of utter calamity, the seas become completely calm.

I picture black skies with intense lightning and rain beating down that change almost in an instant to the amber and orange hues that you'd see at sunset, evoking the whole "red skies at night, sailor's delight" idiom. The instant reversal of the weather system would have been crazily bizarre for the sailors to witness, and this incredible divine intervention by God to alter the weather would have helped seal their conversion to believe in the one true Lord and the God of Jonah. Not only did God use the storm to chase down Jonah by way of a big fish, but he also used it to turn the hearts of Roman enemies of God, to become believers in God and make vows to him. Now that's a divine miracle.

Although written centuries later, Romans 7:15-20 has a very purposeful application to the story of Jonah, as Paul fought the same internal battles that Jonah did. Paul says:

> I do not understand what I do. For what I want to do I do not do, but what I hate I do. And if I do what I do not want to do, I agree that the law is good. As it is, it is no longer I myself who do it, but it is sin living in me. For I know that good itself does not dwell in me, that is, in my sinful nature. For I have the desire to do what is good, but I cannot carry it out. For I do not do the good I want to do, but the evil I do not want to do—this I keep on doing. Now if I do what I do not want to do, it is no longer I who do it, but it is sin living in me that does it.

Can you identify with Paul, Jonah, or the countless other characters in the Bible who know righteousness and truth and what their mission is, yet run in the other direction? I think we all get caught up in moments where we are excited to step up and shine for God, but still we stumble and fall when the going gets tough. We *know* what we should be doing as called followers of God. He presents us with opportunities to love our enemies and further His kingdom work here on Earth, yet we make excuses and turn the other way.

One moment of weakness I can recall personally happened a few months back when I was merging from one highway onto another. I came around a curve, and before me was a guy standing behind his SUV that had just run off the road and into the ditch.

He was waving his arms, trying to get vehicles to stop and help. I was probably cruising a little too fast in the first place, but in a moment of split-second decision-making, I couldn't easily stop; I didn't make an attempt to stop or go back, and I kept driving. I figured, *Someone else will see him and stop to help.* That moment has replayed in my mind dozens of times since. I drive a pickup truck, and I could have possibly helped pull his vehicle back on the street. I carry jumper cables, highway flares, and other tools that I could have used to lend assistance. Or worse yet, if someone had been injured, I could have possibly raced them to the nearest hospital or provided first aid until an ambulance arrived. In hindsight, I chose to avoid the situation because of my own selfish schedule and personal appointments, and I can only hope and pray that the occupants of that vehicle were okay. I hope that God allows me other chances to redeem myself to more wholly serve Him and His people in the future.

Once Jonah was swallowed up and in the belly of the fish, he prayed to God for a second chance. He recognized that running from God was folly and asked for a chance to redeem himself and follow God's mission for him. Jeremiah 23:24 says, "'Can a man hide himself in secret places so that I cannot see him?' declares the Lord. 'Do I not fill heaven and earth?'" Another verse puts it like this: "If I go up to the heavens, you are there; if I make my bed in the depths, you are there" (Psalm 139:8). Jonah knew in his deepest moment of despair that God was going to help him see his mission through by turning the hearts and minds of the people of Nineveh. And you know what? God was with him every step of the way. The fish spit him up three days later, paralleling the three days Jesus would spend in the tomb. And as with Jesus, God never forgot about Jonah, and he rescued him from certain death.

Jonah's mission of preaching to Nineveh went on to be so successful that it saved the entire city from calamity. Even the king took off his robe, put on a sackcloth, and sat in the dust to repent. Jonah, with God's help, had that kind of incredible effect in saving thousands of lives from their impending eternal separation of God.

It's interesting to think about how our lives intertwine with the lives of so many others—an *It's a Wonderful Life* entanglement of sorts. If Jonah had never preached the good news to the Ninevites and encouraged them to turn from their wicked ways, the city of Nineveh might have been destroyed like Sodom and Gomorrah. But God kept his promise, and He spared Nineveh.

Praise God that He used this one man to save not just the city from destruction, but also the sailors aboard the ship bound for Tarshish who came to know God through a miracle on the high seas. We only have so many days on planet Earth. Let us number them and use them wisely to serve our Lord and bring others closer to Him.

CHAPTER 3: MIRACLE OF SAFE PASSAGE

৵৵৽

*"Since you are my rock and my
fortress, for the sake of your name
lead and guide me."* | Psalm 31:3

t's early January, and a young office assistant at a large firm in the city has made a New Year's resolution to more readily offer kindness to strangers in her everyday life. On one particular day, she is running late for her new entry-level position as an office assistant in one of the firm's lower-level offices. A man dressed haphazardly in cheap workout clothes, who does not seem to fit in with the other executives in suits and ties, enters the foyer right behind her. He looks to be hot and sweaty, and his hair is all disheveled. As he steps through the turnstile door, he stumbles and drops his coffee all over the floor. The other executives in the foyer pass on by, but the woman sympathetically stops and kneels down to help the poor man, who is clearly embarrassed and flustered, help clean up the mess. He thanks her for her kindness, and both carry on their separate ways.

It isn't until later in the morning when the young woman is on her way to a meeting and steps inside an elevator that, in an instant, she recognizes the man again. This time, he is fully dressed in a tailored suit and carrying an expensive leather briefcase. The man recognizes her and says he is a brand-new board member at the firm. He explains he was running late, and was on his way up to the executive washroom to shower and change after a morning jog around the city. He hands her a business card with his name on it and says to give him a call if she is ever looking to move up to an executive assistant position.

All because of her moment of kindness and hospitality to help a stranger in their moment of need, her blessing to another became an even greater blessing in return. Now, this story is purely hypothetical, but it's an example of a parable to teach to the tenets of kindness, benevolence, and hospitality.

Mark 4 is a chapter of parables. Jesus often uses parables to guide us, relatable stories that teach a moral or spiritual lesson. Teachers will often incorporate easy-to-understand examples when conveying thoughts and ideas to their students. Many of the examples in Mark 4, for instance, are botany related, since nearly everyone would have had some familiarity with plants, seeds, and nature, being so strongly connected to the agrarian society of the time. Jesus preached the parables found in Mark 4 from a boat, which was probably revolutionary for the time. The boat was anchored just offshore, and the hillside would have made for a natural amphitheater to acoustically carry sound waves of his voice to the hundreds who were gathered on the hillside to hear him speak.

Have you ever heard how well sound carries across water? I live on a small lake and can often hear neighbors across the cove from me talking as if they were standing in my own backyard. (Sometimes, though, you hear a few more details than you care to know . . .) I can clearly hear kids yelling with excitement as they paddle their kayaks or go tubing behind a boat over a half mile away on the main channel. Water helps bounce sound waves along, and without any obstructions like grass, trees, and rocks to muffle and dampen the noise, sound carries particularly well in these conditions.

At the end of the long day, Jesus and the disciples likely needed a break from the people, time to get some food, and a chance to decompress from the day's activities. Jesus said in Mark 4:35, "Let us go over to the other side." But as they were sailing, a ferocious storm squall kicked up, and the waves broke over the boat and threatened to swamp it. Verses 38-40 state:

> Jesus was in the stern, sleeping on a cushion. The disciples woke him and said to him, "Teacher, don't you care if we drown?" He got up, rebuked the wind and said to the waves, "Quiet! Be still!" Then the wind died down and it was completely calm. He said to his disciples, "Why are you so afraid? Do you still have no faith?"

The word of God is true, more solid than any bedrock there ever was. The disciples missed this miracle when Jesus first spoke it. I'll be honest—I've read this story dozens of times and have heard it preached on, and until recently, I've missed it too. The readily apparent, splendid miracle is that Jesus awoke and commanded the storm to be calm, but the **hidden miracle** contained in Mark 4:35 is when Jesus said, "Let us go over to the other side." If Jesus made that statement, it meant they were *absolutely* going to make it to the other side! There was no mistaking it: the boat would not sink or capsize, it wouldn't catch on fire, they would not be eaten by sea serpents, pirates wouldn't intercept and kidnap them, or any other of the hundred other possible scenarios. Jesus wouldn't put them in harm's way if He said they'd make it, and so the miracle was already laid—they would definitely make it through the storm unscathed. He only used the storm as a mode of building their trust in him during their journey, as he taught his disciples to trust his authority and believe in His words.

After the storm, the disciples were likely even more terrified of the God inside their boat than the storm outside it. We need to trust Jesus in the storms of our life. We must believe that if He commands us to do something, we will weather (pun intended) the storms that come our way as we navigate our life's journey. There will always be storms, just like the squall that tossed that little boat on the Sea of Galilee. But we always have His word to fall back on, and His promises never fail. He will lead us and guide us in safe passage, and His word is always true.

CHAPTER 4: A MIRACULOUS FISH STORY

⦁❀⦁

*"Once again, the kingdom of heaven is like
a net that was let down into the lake and
caught all kinds of fish."* | Matthew 13:47

Nope, this isn't another chapter on Jonah. This is a new fish story, because let's face it, can you ever have too many so-*fish*-ticated fish stories? Ugh, cod this get any punnier? Sorry, the jokes don't get any betta than this.

Moving right along . . . I've haddock with these shenanigans!

The setting for this story found in Luke 5 takes place on the Sea of Galilee, where Simon Peter, James, and John were with Jesus while He preached from their fishing boat. After He finished speaking to the crowds, Jesus told them to lower their nets. Simon begrudgingly did, stating that he and his guys had fished all night but had no luck. Out of respect for Jesus, however, he did what was commanded of him. The instructions of Jesus might seem silly to us, but it's important to remember that His ways are not our ways, and the results of our obedience are much more incredible than we can possibly wrap our minds around.

Upon casting out their nets again, Jesus provided an overabundance of fish up to the brim of each net, which is an incredible miracle. Verses 6 and 7 describe the haul of fish being so large, the first boat began to sink! They signaled for their friends to come and help them in a second boat. Wow. Now that's a fish story if I ever heard one—one that's completely true and free from exaggeration!

But this begs the question, is there a **hidden miracle** here as to what happened to all of those fish? It's likely that Zebedee was at the age where he couldn't physically run the fishing operation to the extent that he could in his younger years. To make matters worse, he had just lost three of his young, spry fishermen to follow Jesus into ministry—James, John, and Simon Peter. Although it's speculative, I believe that the profits from this dramatic haul of fish served two purposes: to solidify Zebedee's faith (and that of any onlookers who witnessed the event), and to financially sustain the business from the loss of three of its employees to keep the business afloat (pun intended) until replacement staff could be hired and trained.

One thing that bristles me a bit is when people say that God sustained them through their moments of hardship. But think about that: it comes nowhere near close enough to describing the miraculous abundance God regularly so generously gives. "Sustaining," to me, seems evocative of floating in the ocean following a shipwreck, a situation where God is helping a person to just barely keep their head above water, but that's about it. Or perhaps like living on life support, just barely ticking along but nothing more. But that's never been my experience in life; I believe God not only just "sustains us" but almost always gives us excess, a superfluous, overflowing abundance if we pray for it and ask Him for help.

To further prove this point, take two other great stories of miracle provisions that are found in 2 Kings 4:1-7. In the first story, we read the story of the widow's olive oil:

The wife of a man from the company of the prophets cried out to Elisha, "Your servant my husband is dead, and you know that he revered the Lord. But now his creditor is coming to take my two boys as his slaves." Elisha replied to her, "How can I help you? Tell me, what do you have in your house?" "Your servant has nothing there at all," she said, "except a small jar of olive oil." Elisha said, "Go around and ask all your neighbors for empty jars. Don't ask for just a few. Then go inside and shut the door behind you and your sons. Pour oil into all the jars, and as each is filled, put it to one side." She left him and shut the door behind her and her sons. They brought the jars to her and she kept pouring. When all the jars were full, she said to her son, "Bring me another one." But he replied, "There is not a jar left." Then the oil stopped flowing. She went and told the man of God, and he said, "Go, sell the oil and pay your debts. You and your sons can live on what is left."

The woman was destitute. Elisha was a prophet from God and had the ability to help the woman. God provided through Elisha and not only met the woman's needs, but the oil kept pouring until she could fill every jar she could get her hands on. Abundance to the ma. I love the framework in this story where it's specifically the *widow* who pours the oil into the jars that she would in turn be able to sell for money, not Elisha. If it were Elisha who poured them, the widow would be inclined to give her thanks to Elisha. But the Lord clearly demonstrated that it was His power that provided providence in her time of need.

The very next part of this same chapter tells the story of the Shunammite woman and her blessing of hospitality to Elisha as he traveled:

One day Elisha went to Shunem. And a well-to-do woman was there, who urged him to stay for a meal. So whenever he came

by, he stopped there to eat. She said to her husband, "I know that
this man who often comes our way is a holy man of God. Let's
make a small room on the roof and put in it a bed and a table,
a chair and a lamp for him. Then he can stay there whenever
he comes to us." One day when Elisha came, he went up to his
room and lay down there. He said to his servant Gehazi, "Call
the Shunammite." So he called her, and she stood before him.
Elisha said to him, "Tell her, 'You have gone to all this trouble
for us. Now what can be done for you?'" (2 Kings 4:8-13)

Once again, we see a beautiful act of kindness in providing help
during a time of need. The woman noticed Elisha's need, told her
husband that they should build a little apartment up on their roof
whenever Elisha passed through their town so he'd have a place
to crash, they did so, and God met Elisha's needs. They didn't just
offer Elisha a to-go meal, toss a few coins in his direction to buy
a cheeseburger with, or a one-time gift of lodging. God, using the
Shunammite family as his instrument, and blessed Elisha with a
furnished apartment and multiple meals. Probably even cable tele-
vision and a comfy duvet comforter, too. I'm speculating on those
last two amenities, though; I wasn't there.

Lastly, let's look at the example of prayer that's found in Job
1:5. Job often prayed and praised God the morning after his sons
and daughters would hold raucous parties and soirees. He prayed
for things unseen and unrealized:

When a period of feasting had run its course, Job would make
arrangements for them to be purified. Early in the morning he
would sacrifice a burnt offering for each of them, thinking,
"Perhaps my children have sinned and cursed God in their
hearts." This was Job's regular custom.

I often pray to God myself, "Thank you for the blessings you've given me, including the things I'm unaware of, don't recognize, or take for granted," which is similar to Job's prayer. Innocent, sustaining prayers during moments of need. Prayers of thanks for meeting even my unrecognized needs.

Zebedee's fishing operation is no different, and I don't think Jesus had any intention of letting this business fail with the departure of three of its most experienced staff. He wanted it to thrive long after James, John, and Simon Peter left to follow Jesus in his ministry. Let us remember to thank God for abundant blessings that give us more than enough, as well as for the blessings and grace He bestows for things that we don't readily recognize but are graciously gifted nonetheless.

Whether God blesses His children with manna and quail in the wilderness, performs the miracle of turning water into wine, or feeds a crowd with a few loaves of bread and a couple of fish, there is always abundance and much left over. God is generous, abundantly good, and provides sustenance for our minds, bodies, and souls, just like He provisioned righteous Zebedee and his fishing operation with an unanticipated haul of fish.

CHAPTER 5: A MIRACULOUS GIFT THAT KEEPS ON GIVING

*"No one will be able to stand against you
all the days of your life. As I was with
Moses, so I will be with you; I will never
leave you nor forsake you."* | Joshua 1:5

Have you ever had a barrier in your life you could not pass or overcome? Perhaps it was an impediment to personal growth, spiritual growth, professional or career advancement, or a physical feat you hoped to achieve but just were not able to. Last summer, some dear neighborhood friends along with my parents and I tried our hand at "Blackbeard's Revenge," an escape room in St. Louis. We are all intelligent people capable of problem-solving and overcoming puzzles, so we figured this would be a cinch. The difficulty rating was only "medium" and the pass rate was 63 percent, so surely, we thought, we would be able to complete the challenge of finding Blackbeard's treasure hidden inside a mysterious Aztec temple.

The guide running the escape room told us if we held up the "I'm stumped" card to the camera, she would give us three clues along the way if we needed them. And if we really got stuck, we could always ask for more, rather than just wallowing in the room not having any fun. Well, the escape room humbled all of us—

while we were able to unlock the challenges to advance us from the first room to the second, we never even made it to the third room. We hit all sorts of barriers and walls (both literal and figurative) during our hour-long quest, and we used all of our free hints plus another three just to get that far. Not exactly a stellar example of our problem-solving. Finally, our time was up, and we had to leave the challenge without completing the puzzle.

Now, how does this relate to the Bible's miracles? Later in his life, post-Egypt and the parting of the Red Sea, we learn about the Exodus 34 story of Moses and the veil, a barrier of sorts that creates a certain separation. Moses had just trekked up Mount Sinai for the second time to receive another copy of the Ten Commandments. Upon returning down the mountain the first time, Moses saw that the Israelites had built a golden calf and were worshiping it. In anger and frustration, he smashed the first set of stone tablets. To give a little background, verses 29-35 explains:

> When Moses came down from Mount Sinai with the two tablets of the covenant law in his hands, he was not aware that his face was radiant because he had spoken with the Lord. When Aaron and all the Israelites saw Moses, his face was radiant, and they were afraid to come near him. But Moses called to them; so Aaron and all the leaders of the community came back to him, and he spoke to them. Afterward all the Israelites came near him, and he gave them all the commands the Lord had given him on Mount Sinai.

> When Moses finished speaking to them, he put a veil over his face. But whenever he entered the Lord's presence to speak with him, he removed the veil until he came out. And when he came out and told the Israelites what he had been commanded, they saw that his face was radiant. Then Moses would put the veil back over his face until he went in to speak with the Lord.

We don't know exactly what the radiant glow on Moses' face looked like, nor what kind of veil Moses wore, but it is apparent that Moses' presence in front of God transferred a certain holiness or glow to him that was enough to spook even his own brother, Aaron.

In the most basic terms, a veil is a shroud or covering that shields the face. Most people are familiar with a bridal veil, which evolved out of a superstition that the husband should not see the bride's face before the pronouncement that they were man and wife. Later in history, the veil came to symbolize "modesty and obedience," which is the same reverence that Moses offered God. Moses could lift his veil in the presence of God, but among the Israelites, the purity and holiness that transferred and was reflected from God to Moses was too great for the people to gaze upon.

While the veil of Moses in Exodus created a barrier between God and the people, praise God for removing the barrier between God and Man. Matthew 27 details the final hours of Jesus hanging on the cross, and in verse 51 we learn that at the very moment Jesus yielded his life and died, "the curtain of the temple was torn in two from top to bottom." The New King James Bible version translates the verse quite literally as "the veil was torn in two."

Herein, is where we discover a **hidden miracle**. The veil of Moses was a barrier, a separation between God and man. But following Christ dying for our sins on the cross, no longer was a veil of separation needed or even required. Hebrews 10:19-20 (NKJV) says, "Therefore, brethren, having boldness to enter the Holiest by the blood of Jesus, by a new and living way which He consecrated for us, through the *veil*, that is, His flesh." The Holy Spirit lives within all of us through Jesus' sacrifice.

The secret of bridging the gap and having full access to God without a veil or barrier is obedience, and as author Andrew Murray explains, "The secret of true obedience [. . .] is a clear and close personal relationship with God. All of our attempts to achieve full obedience will fail until we have access to His abiding fellowship."Once we have that relationship of obedience, we may enjoy a type of communion with God that the Israelites of the Old Testament never had the benefit of experiencing.

The veil is lifted, the curtain is torn in two—a miracle feat only possible through Jesus dying for our sins on the cross. No longer is intercession from a Holy Priest like Moses required. My encouragement to you is to strive for obedience to seek full access to God, barrier-free, through prayer and study. Our access to Him is His gift to us.

CHAPTER 6: THE MIRACLE OF SECOND CHANCES

.๏ะ ๑.

"I love to tell the story of unseen things above,
of Jesus and His glory, of Jesus and His love."
"I Love to Tell the Story"
Kate Hankey (1866) / William Fischer (1869)

Have you ever been offered a do-over, or a second chance to make something right? A chance to do something better? Sometimes those things work to our advantage, and sometimes circumstances will hand us a "game over," leaving us to try again next season or next year, or perhaps grant us no further opportunity at all.

Maybe your second chance was missing the shot at the trophy buck you were after, only to miss because your gun wasn't sighted properly, so now you'll have to wait until your next hunting trip or possibly until next season. Maybe a regret is that you failed to ask your crush to the school dance in time, only to have someone else sweep in and ask them out instead, missing your chance. Maybe you had a major life-saving surgery, one that has given you a new outlook and a new lease on life. Whatever the circumstances may be, we sometimes get second chances at things, and other times our opportunity is lost for good.

As mentioned in a previous chapter, God gave Moses the Ten

Commandments, but did you ever wonder why God etched the commandments on two separate tablets? It wasn't because God couldn't squeeze the font size small enough to fit on one stone, or that He couldn't figure out how to get the Xerox machine to print in duplex on the back of the stone tablet. It is because the first set of commandments is a covenant between God and man, and the second set reflects the relationship between man and man.

Later in the New Testament, when asked what the greatest commandment was, Jesus said, "'Love the Lord your God with all your heart and with all your soul and with all your mind.' This is the first and greatest commandment. And the second is like it: 'Love your neighbor as yourself'" (Matthew 22:37-39). Jesus basically summed up each of the two original tablets: love God, and love others.

It's also important to note that when Jesus spoke the command of loving our neighbors as ourselves, he intended for us to love ourselves first. It is impossible to honor the command of loving our neighbors unless we first have a healthy self-esteem—not in an egocentric, self-absorbed way, but to ensure our maturity and stability. Once we are grounded in our own self-confidence, we can more effectively love others and honor this command.

Galatians 5:22-23 expresses the fruit of the spirit as "love, joy, peace, forbearance, kindness, goodness, faithfulness, gentleness, and self-control. Against such things there is no law." Notice how "love" is first on that list. Love is the guiding principle of all fruit, and John 14 speaks to the holy feature that disciples will be known by their love. These are the tenets of living in step with God.

The **hidden miracle** here is that God is a God of second chances, forgiveness, and love. Both in his physical interaction with Moses, and with the verbal response from Jesus. There aren't too many gifts we receive that are also challenges, but the Ten Commandments are both. All of the commandments hinge on God's greatest gift and His greatest challenge to each one of us: to simply love. After Moses smashed the first set of commandments out of frustration and anger, God offered him a second chance. In fact, we could dissect this that a little further and say that God isn't a God of *second* chances so much that he's a God of *another* chance. God's love is constant, even after our love wavers, is driven by emotion, and fails time and again.

Can you think of some Bible heroes who were given another chance, another opportunity to earn His trust back? A few that come to my mind are Jonah, Mark, Samson, David, Zacchaeus, and Peter. When we have wronged someone, we have no right to *demand* another chance—but we should work to *earn* another chance by our continued demonstration of repentance and change.

Which brings about the providence of Jesus. Jesus is not a "second chance" at Adam, as He is sometimes described, but instead is an intermediary who died for our sins, and in whom we can find salvation if we become baptized believers of Jesus Christ. God does everything possible to draw us to repentance, offering forgiveness and more chances when we falter. In 2 Peter 3:9 it says, "The Lord is not slow in keeping His promise, as some understand slowness. Instead He is patient with you, not wanting anyone to perish, but everyone to come to repentance." If we continue to reject Him, though, we will run out of opportunities and our time here on Earth will expire.

God's grace is our model. We can be repentant ourselves and offer additional chances, forgiveness, and grace to others, just as God offers those blessings to us.

CHAPTER 7: A WEDDING MIRACLE

❧☙

*"O God, you are my God, earnestly I seek
you; my soul thirsts for you, my body longs
for you, in a dry and weary land."* | Psalm 63:1

D o you typically give pretty good wedding gifts? I'm embarrassed to admit it, but in hindsight, one of the worst wedding gifts I ever gave was at the wedding of an old high school friend who got married in Austin, Texas, about fifteen years ago. I was a poor, lowly copilot in my first commuter airline job at the time and not making much money. I hadn't been to too many weddings at that point in my life, either, so I was less than versed on proper etiquette. After accounting for my travel expenses from home to Texas, a rental car, and lodging for two nights in an upscale boutique hotel where the wedding took place, the costs were really racking up. They say that the price of a wedding gift should at least equal the approximate cost of the meal to the host, but I could only afford a bottle of wine and some relatively inexpensive kitchen scissors or something pretty lame from the bride and groom's Target guest registry. It wasn't much, and thankfully my gift-giving has gotten a little better and more creative since. But as a young guy just finding my way in my mid-twenties, that was what it was.

In the book of John 2, the stage is set for a beautiful garden wedding in Cana. We know that Jesus, His mother, and His disciples were all invited. I'm sure there was plenty of food, laughs, and dancing that night, and probably a few embarrassing stories told, too, as those have a way of resurfacing around family and friends. The servants would have been busy hustling and bustling about to make sure the guests were well attended to and that every detail was in perfect order.

Jesus' mother came up to Him after a little while and said, "There is no more wine." The New King James translation is even starker, stating, "They have no wine," as if perhaps that important detail was overlooked in the first place (John 2:3).

As a side note, I've always found it interesting that no one explicitly told Jesus what to do; they only presented him with their problem. There is a lesson to be learned here that should translate to our daily prayer life, where I'll admit I sometimes try to "micromanage" my prayers. Instead of simply laying my problem at Jesus' feet and allowing Him to do with it as is His will, I'll pray for the details of how to accomplish or overcome the challenge that I'm facing. It's good to have plans, ideas, and a course of action and not just simply petition or request things while you sit idly by with your arms folded or twiddling your thumbs, of course. But in truth, we needn't get too involved in the fine details of our prayers. Matthew 6:8 says, "Your father knows what you need before you ask Him," so we should be more concerned with ensuring we are walking in step with God rather than trying to tell Him what to do to make everything in our lives happy and right again, per our limited vision.

So, when the problem was laid at Jesus' feet regarding the lack of wine, Jesus told the servants to fill six stone jars nearby with water. These water vessels were intended for ceremonious washing, each holding from twenty to thirty gallons. They were filled to the brim, and when the master of the wedding banquet came and tasted the water that Jesus had transformed into wine, he was greatly impressed by the choice of wine. We see honor in this story in Jesus honoring His mother. The servants honored and obeyed the request to fill and transport 250-pound jars of water in the hot desert when they could not yet see what the purpose would be. And Jesus honored his Father as well when he said "the time has not yet come" but saw an opportunity to serve, honor, and love and took it.

A preacher can do a much better job than I can of drawing connections between how these were religious/ceremonious jars and the literary allusion of how water being changed to wine is divinely connected to the blood of Jesus, as well as explaining the importance that this was Jesus' first recorded miracle. Or maybe the counter-cultural fact that the jars were used for washing the outside of the body, but Jesus would transform the water into wine that would go inside the body—just the first of many examples where Jesus would flip on its head the ways and methods of public thinking at the time. But for the **hidden miracle** purposes of this chapter, I'm fascinated as to how Jesus provided enough wine for this banquet that it would have filled approximately 750 typical wine bottles as we know them today.

Biblical weddings typically lasted several days, and we know that when Jesus performed this miracle it was already the "third day," meaning only a few more days were left before the Sabbath. Now, this might have been one heck of a wedding, but even if there were several hundred guests, it's unlikely that the wine supply was all lapped up during that week. Remember back to Chapter 4: God rarely simply *sustains*. He almost always provides an *overabundance*!

The obvious miracle here is the transformation of water into wine and how Jesus possesses power over science, modifying the molecular structure of the water to bypass grape growth and maturation on the vine, picking, pressing, and fermenting. But the underlying **hidden miracle** is that Jesus provides—and provides abundantly. The wedding couple was probably able to sell some of the additional unused wine to help support them as they were first starting out in life, or they may have been able to save it for their own consumption in the future since wine was very much a staple of mealtime during ancient Biblical times. God not only gives, but gives abundantly—not just barely enough to get through the rest of a wedding week that was already half over.

Now that was one heck of a miracle wedding gift—much nicer than a single bottle of mediocre Midwest wine and some lousy kitchen shears.

CHAPTER 8: MIRACLE SMOKE FROM A DISTANT FIRE

.୦୧ ଈଲ.

"After the earthquake came a fire, but the Lord was not in the fire. And after the fire came a gentle whisper." | 1 Kings 19:12

The book of John contains the accounts of Peter's three denials of Jesus. After Peter famously stated that he would never turn his back on Jesus, John 18 sets the stage for the three times that Peter ended up denying the Lord. Verse 18 may seem pretty mundane, but I have found an important connection between this verse and another small detail just a few chapters later that connects back to it.

Just after Peter denied Jesus the first time, John 18:18 states, "It was cold, and the servants and officials stood around a fire they had made to keep warm. Peter also was standing with them, warming himself." The Bible never minces words, and nearly everything holds a multifaceted meaning. This particular verse that seems fairly mundane does, in fact, importantly link to another verse post-crucifixion.

Pause for a second, though. Have you ever stood around a campfire? Think of the sensory elements associated with an outdoor wood-burning fire: the flicker of the flame, the warmth of the heat, the crackle of the logs. Where there's fire, there's smoke. The smell of a distant fire has the power to transport me back to my Boy Scout days growing up in Pennsylvania, hiking and camping in the Appalachian Mountains when we would have campfires at night to relax around after walking many miles during the day. I also love the ethereal way that smoke sometimes hangs in the valley on a still, calm evening just before sunset. Try to picture the angelic way a late afternoon light glistens through the trees and catches the haze of smoke in the air. The English language doesn't have a word to adequately describe it, but the Japanese call this dappled light "*komorebi.*" It looks mystical, magical, and peaceful.

A campfire has a way of taking us back to a time and place, and Peter would soon remember the campfire he stood around a few days earlier that was recorded in John 18:18. John 21 tells us that Jesus had just been crucified. With their Messiah's death, the oppressive Roman government still in power, and with one of their own, Judas, dead from suicide, the disciples were completely drained. Their lives as they had known them had been upended. Eager anticipation of a political revolution was crushed. They felt hopeless, afraid, and dejected, and so they turned back to their former lives as fishermen as a means of escape, reverting to what was familiar and comfortable to them.

We all have the propensity to return to what feels comfortable when we are stressed and feel overwhelmed. That's why comfort food is such a delicious draw. It's not possible to have a big supper at Cracker Barrel and not feel at least some of your stress melt away.

I can completely understand the disciples' despair, as I've had many times in my life where my interpersonal relationships have beat me down so bad that I've directed my energy into my work and picked up extra work trips that took me out of town for a few days. I used that as a means to get away for a bit, clear my head, and focus my energy on something else. At other times in my life, I've felt more like staying closer to home and focusing on being alone in nature by doing an activity I enjoy, such as going for a hike, a solitary kayak paddle, or casting my line into the lake for a little fishing. Peter found a connection between his favorite pastime and his career and had made commercial fishing his labor of love. Under great stress, uncertainty, and hopelessness, he understandably returned to what he enjoyed and poured his energy into his recreation and trade.

After the disciples had finished fishing and were heading to shore, John 21:9 says, "When they landed, they saw a fire of burning coals there with fish on it, and some bread. Jesus said to them, 'Bring some of the fish you have just caught.' Peter was overjoyed to see Jesus, and exclaimed, 'It is the Lord!'" Once he got to shore, Peter would have noticed the fire, the flames, the flicker of the embers, and the smoke. The **hidden miracle** here is that Peter would have smelled the smoke and instantly been transported back to that moment a few days prior when he had just denied Jesus—that very moment in time when it was cold and he was standing around a fire, warming himself.

What a complex mix of emotions Peter would have felt in that moment on the shore, seeing Jesus again. He loved the Lord but had denied the Lord. He was overjoyed at seeing his greatest friend following His miraculous resurrection, but he was also wracked by the guilt and shame of hurting him by denying even their slightest acquaintance. Author Tim Ferrara explains that despite the struggles that inevitably arise between two humans, Christians need to be built up and encouraged by one another, and he goes on to say that "the Christian walk is hard enough without the enemy trying to thwart us at every step. We need encouragement from like-minded believers in Christ who will be there to pray with us, encourage us, and strengthen us." And that's exactly what Jesus did.

After they brought the boat to shore, Jesus asked Peter three times, "Do you love me [. . .]?" And Peter responded yes each time. Jesus used the fine detail of smoke to connect his mind to that time and place. But an even greater miracle is that Jesus offered redemption to Peter by asking Peter three times if he loved him, and extended to Peter His grace and forgiveness. Those three reaffirming questions offset the three denials by Peter, assuring him that his sins were forgiven and the relationship was mended. Peter was reinstated as a full disciple of Jesus, their connection completely restored.

Until this exchange, Peter had yet to fully grasp that if there is one overarching theme in his relationship with Jesus, it is certainly the power of God's love for every one of us. In His perfect love, He created the world and everything in it. He offers mankind grace despite our repeated rebellion. God's love sent Jesus down from Heaven as our Redeemer to rescue us, and that same love raised Jesus from the dead on the third day (1 Corinthians 15:4). His love is preparing a place for us by His side at this very moment (John 14:3). Jesus and His love for us will return and rescue us to dine with Him in the banquet room of heaven one day. Jesus loved Peter, despite his shortcomings and fallacies, in the same way that he loves you and me.

Just like Peter, I'm thankful that my heavenly father extends His grace and forgiveness to me when I stumble as well. Let us learn from our mistakes when we blunder, offer repentance, ask for forgiveness, and continue to move forward in the mission field.

CHAPTER 9: MIRACULOUS PROMISE BEFORE THE PLAN

_᎒Ꭷ᎒Ꭷ᎒_

"Have no fear, little flock; have no fear, little flock,
for the Father has chosen to give you the kingdom;
have no fear, little flock."
"Have No Fear, Little Flock"

'm a planner—it's just a part of my nature. Whenever I go on a vacation, I like to have an itinerary of sorts ready to go so that as soon as I arrive, I can hit the ground running. I don't like to be the guy fumbling around at the brochure rack in the motel trying to figure out what I want to go see or do; I'd much rather do my research and legwork in advance. Now that's not to say that plans can't change a bit. Weather can throw a wrench into even the best-laid plans, and sometimes I'll feel up to doing one thing over another, so I'll swap the day's activities. While I have no promises or assurances that my plans won't go awry, a plan is at least in place.

In Joshua 6, we read the familiar story of Joshua and the battle of Jericho. God commanded Joshua and the Israelites to walk around the city six times and, on the seventh day, to march around the city seven times, blowing the trumpets and ram's horns. This famous biblical story is often recounted in vacation Bible school programs, which is probably where I first heard it. The song "Joshua Fought the Battle of Jericho" has had many adaptations over the centuries, from its beginnings as an old plantation slave song to a famous version by Elvis Presley in 1960, but this story's purpose is to teach the lessons of obedience to God and the importance of following God's instructions to ensure a successful, lasting victory in the end.

It is in verse 2 that we discover a **hidden miracle**. Then the Lord said to Joshua, "See, I have delivered Jericho into your hands, along with its king and its fighting men." Even before God gave the instructions of *when* to march or when to blow the ram's horns and trumpets, he *already* promised victory by speaking in past tense. Similar to our example in Chapter 3 where Jesus gave the disciples the promise of safe passage so they never actually had to worry about the storm getting in their way, God immediately promised the Israelites victory over Jericho. Like many times in the Bible, it wasn't until after the miracle was already promised that the plan was revealed.

God knows the outcome of the game before the first quarter has even started, before the team has come out of the locker room, before the cheerleaders stretch, and before a single second has ticked off the clock. I think I'll pick God's side in this game of life that we're playing, a victory assured. Blow the ram's horn, let's get ready to rumble.

CHAPTER 10: MIRACULOUS ALLUSIONS TO EDEN

ᴥᴥ

"This is my Father's world: The birds their carols raise,
the morning light, the lily white, declare their Maker's praise."
"This is My Father's World"
Maltbie Davenport Babcock, 1901

'm no green thumb, but I do like to dabble in some horticulture projects around my house each year. I'll often take a trip to a nursery or garden center to see all of the beautiful annuals and perennials, and usually I can't help but buy a few to add to my gardens. I find beauty in God's creation, whether it's in my yard, at an arboretum or botanical garden, or while out in nature during a hike in the forest or meadow. There's a sense of peace that comes over me when I can wake up in the morning, have my coffee on my back deck, and watch the hummingbirds and butterflies visit the plants in my yard, enjoying the beauty of the flowers just as much as I am.

If I ever came into a large windfall of money, I've often dreamed that it would be fun to build a National Bible Prayer Garden and Winery, a place that incorporates many of the over one hundred plants that are either mentioned in the Bible or common throughout the Holy Lands. A place with a little white chapel as the focal point in the middle that anyone would be free to visit, and with trails that wind through the gardens and vineyards with benches along the way to sit and pray or just bask in God's presence. If I could add a few animals to this hypothetical scenario, it would be about as idyllic and close to the garden of Eden as you could get this side of heaven.

In his paper "Creation's Original Diet and the Changes at the Fall," author Jim Stambaugh states, "One must, in humble obedience, simply believe God at His word. God, through His Word, clearly shows that the original, created creatures were to eat only plants." As crazy as it might seem to us in this day and age, Adam and Eve likely had nothing to fear in the Garden of Eden by either petting a tiger or scratching a bear behind its ears. The animals simply didn't see them as dinner.

Dr. Nathaniel T. Jeanson of the Institute for Creation Research proposes that anatomical and physiological features, such as the jaws and teeth on a sabertooth tiger, might have been used for multiple purposes. While possibly originally used for eating large pieces of fruit or breaking open large seeds, later those same teeth would have served the purpose of pursuing and eating carnivorous prey. Genesis 1:29-30 explains it a bit further:

> Then God said, 'Behold, I have given you every plant yielding seed that is on the surface of the earth, and every tree yielding seed: it shall be food for you; and to every beast of the earth and to every bird of the sky and to everything that moves on the earth that has life, I have given every green plant for food:' and it was so.

It wasn't until after Noah and the ark came to rest on Mount Ararat that God permitted the eating of meat, given as a concession to the sinfulness of man. After the Great Flood, both man and animals were permitted to eat meat.

Later in the Old Testament, Isaiah 11:6-7 states, "The wolf will live with the lamb, the leopard will lie down with the goat, the calf and the lion and the yearling together; and a little child will lead them. The cow will feed with the bear, their young will lie down together, and the lion will eat straw like the ox." Let us also consider Isaiah 65:25 that similarly states, "The wolf and the lamb will feed together, and the lion will eat straw like the ox, and dust will be the serpent's food."

That means that Isaiah's prophecy is yet another subtle **hidden miracle**—not just some random prediction, but an allusion to the garden of Eden. In the first moments after creation, before sin entered the world, man had nothing to fear from any animal; there was no predator-prey relationship present, as all creatures fed on plants. Thus, Isaiah is clearly referencing the garden of Eden in these passages. One day, all humans and animals will go back to a plant diet, as was ordained from the beginning. So, in the future, petting a lion or hugging a bear might be possible!

One day, the original plan will be restored. How cool it is that the prophet Isaiah reminds us of that promise of old.

CHAPTER 11: MIRACLE OF RADIANCE

.ⱥℰ 𝔤ₐ.

"Hide it under a bushel? No!
I'm going to let it shine,
let it shine, all the time, let it shine."
"This Little Light of Mine" (unattributed)

What's the brightest light you've ever seen? I instantly think of an arc welder's light that requires a special lens to view to keep it from burning your retina. Sunshine pop group The Visions (how ironic a name) sang a song back in 1967 called "Keepin' Your Eyes on the Sun." It's a catchy little upbeat tune, but 0 out of 10 doctors and moms recommend looking at the sun with your naked eyes for real.

A few years ago in 2017, I got to witness a total solar eclipse. I drove two hours south of where I live to be directly under its path, and it was one of the neatest things I've ever seen. I remember the shadow of the eclipse approaching across the fields and how the crickets began chirping, thinking it was nightfall. The breeze kicked up due to the differential heating of the rural surrounding farmland, with the ominous forbearance that something big was about to happen. The sky darkened enough that many stars could be seen during the middle of the day, which totally blew my mind. The coolest part, though, was wearing these special glasses that local stores and businesses gave away in the days leading up to the eclipse so that you could watch the moon pass directly between the Earth and the sun, casting its shadow on us all. How cool that God gives us a rare treat like a solar eclipse to witness the brilliant artistry of His creative hand.

Besides the sun, another bright light of sorts is recorded in the Bible. Way back at the beginning of his life, we see in Exodus 2:2 that Moses' mother recognized from his infancy that he was "good." Pharaoh had just decreed that all newborn sons must be killed (sounds a lot like Herod's infanticide to kill all newborn boys during the time of Jesus, doesn't it? What's with these insecure kings and murder?!). So Moses' mother, Jochebed, hid him for three months. After three months, he had grown too big to hide anymore, so Moses' mother dropped him in a wicker basket and placed him in the bulrushes along the Nile River while his sister, Miriam, watched in the distance. Moses would later be discovered by Pharaoh's own daughter, who rescued and raised him in the home of the richest family on Earth at the time, before later delivering the Israelite people from Egyptian oppression and slavery decades later.

It's interesting to note that the idea of "good" or "fine" in reference to Moses is the same adjective "good" from the Hebrew "*tov*" found in the creation account. Genesis 1:3-4 says, "And God said, 'Let there be light,' and there was light. God saw that the light was good, and He separated the light from the darkness." The **hidden miracle** in this story is that we can surmise that Moses had a special light or radiance about him when he was born (different from the light discussed a few chapters ago that he received while communing with God as an adult). Jochebed recognized that Moses was "good" and divinely appointed, and she knew she must do anything she could to ensure her son's vitality. A mother always knows!

It's also important to keep in mind that while John 8:12 describes Jesus as the "Light of the World," on this side of heaven, many good things also take place at night.

- When God's presence was over the waters in Genesis 1, He created both night and day, both intertwined so they could equally complement each other.

- The body is rested and restored, and sleep is typically done at night.

- Psalm 19:1-2 tells us that "knowledge" is oftentimes "revealed" to us at night. I know that's true. Oh, how often I've lain awake at night, unable to sleep, because my mind won't shut off.

- Job 12:22 says, "He reveals the deep things of darkness and brings utter darkness into the light."

- God brought Abraham out of his tent at night to show him the Milky Way and to tell him his descendants would be more numerous than the uncountable stars, a fascinating personal reflective moment in the vastness of a still, desolate desert (Genesis 26:4)

- During the Israelites' time in the wilderness, it was during the nighttime that the manna came down from heaven (Numbers 11:9).

- Hebrew tradition is that sundown marks the start of the next day; quite literally, the "dawn of a new day" begins with darkness.

- Nicodemus came to Jesus at night searching for knowledge and truth (Matthew 27:57).

- It was during the "fourth watch" (between the hours of 3:00 a.m. and 6:00 a.m.) that Jesus walked on water and appeared to the disciples, telling them to be of good cheer and not to be afraid (Matthew 14:25, NKJV).

Good things happen at night! But Revelation 22:5 speaks of a day that is coming when darkness will be no more: "There will be no more night. They will not need the light of a lamp or the light of the sun, for the Lord God will give them light. And they will reign for ever and ever."

I think about flying over the rivers of the Midwest, when I can look down on the Illinois River or the Missouri or Mississippi Valley. At night, you often cannot see exactly where the rivers meander because it's pitch-black, but when the towboats pushing barges up and down the river blast their giant spotlights, it illuminates the entire riverway. It's a stark comparison to the lonely darkness that otherwise befalls the river at night. How much brighter Jesus is than any tugboat spotlight.

At the beginning of Jesus' life when Simeon took the newborn Jesus into his arms, he declared that Jesus was "a light for revelation to the Gentiles, and for glory to Your people Israel" (Luke 2:32). Then, at the end of Jesus' life, darkness was cast over the Earth for three hours while Jesus hung on the cross, but in that darkness was the dawn of the light of salvation (Mark 15:33). Quite literally, Jesus was a beacon of light coming into this world, and He was a beacon of light that cut through utter darkness during his crucifixion. 2 Corinthians 4:6 promises, "For God, who said, 'Let light shine out of darkness,' made his light shine in our hearts to give us the light of the knowledge of God's glory displayed in the face of Christ."

In Genesis 1:3 God commanded, "Let there be light," on the first day, but did you ever wonder how that could be when God didn't create the sun or stars until the fourth day? It wasn't literal sunlight as we know it, but rather a supernatural manifestation of goodness—God's own presence. No matter how much evil abounds, the light of God has permeated from the beginning of time. A new day is coming, Zechariah 14:7 says: "It will be a unique day—a day known only to the LORD—with no distinction between day and night. When evening comes, there will be light." On that day, "even the darkness will not be dark to you; the night will shine like the day, for darkness is as light to you" (Psalm 139:12).

When the outcome of a problem seems like a dead-end street, God often provides a way. He did it for Moses, and the promise of His light in our lives shows He is right there alongside us, too. Like Jesus, Moses had a light in him that could not be extinguished from the moment he was born. God ordained this in Moses' life by using a member of Pharaoh's own royal family, his daughter, to care for Moses in his infancy. The very enemy who had tried (and successfully failed) to kill Moses and the Israelites was the same royal family who raised Moses and cared for him during his youth. God used evil in the form of Pharaoh for good, to glorify His name.

We all have a light about us in the form of the Holy Spirit that enables us to shine for Jesus and honor Him in all that we do, one that can never be snuffed out.

CHAPTER 12: THE MIRACLE WITHIN

.ക ഇ.

"If you love me, keep my commands." | John 14:15

Have you ever noticed how you might be good at something that someone else might be totally adverse to? I've been an airline pilot for over fifteen years, and the challenge of navigating around thunderstorms or taxiing in some of the busiest and most complex airports in the world doesn't faze me. In fact, descending through the clouds with only a half mile of forward visibility safely onto a snow-packed runway at 150 miles per hour is a rush of excitement that completely energizes my being. I have full confidence in the skills I've acquired and the ability of the machines I fly. On the other hand, some travelers are white-knuckled the moment they walk onto a jet as a passenger—even on a clear, sunny day, before the plane has even left the gate.

By the same token, I have almost zero mechanical ability. When my 737 has a mechanical issue that requires us to return to the terminal, when my pickup truck gets a flat tire, or when my laptop computer locks up, I get irritated and frustrated, and it drives me crazy because repair ability is not in my realm of understanding or patience. I love technology, but I get impatient and frustrated when things fail to work as they were designed to do. However, I'm thankful that there are mechanics, technicians, and repair people who do have the skills and talents needed to solve these types of problems.

The innate gifts that the Holy Spirit gives to each of us are SO much better than any gift a human being could impart. James 1:17 says "Every good and perfect gift is from above." Spirit-blessed gifts are given to the church—the body of Christ—so we can empower, build up, and support one another. Like Esau, who was a skillful hunter, and Jacob, who was content to stay at home among the tents and make stew, we all have something important to offer.

It is curious to note that while the Holy Spirit doesn't play "favorites" or give superiority to one person or another, these gifts tend to be in line with a person's particular skills, talents, and personality so that they may be embodied to the fullest. While God gives a variety of gifts, we all have the same Spirit. He is like a parent who loves all of their children equally; they will typically give different Christmas or birthday presents to each of their children that are in line with each child's personality and cognitive level, but each child is valued for who they uniquely are. That's the **hidden miracle** found in James 1:17—we all have distinct God-given talents and skills, and we are all unique in our specific abilities. Our abilities and talents are completely distinct from those of our brethren, and our aptitude and potential is given so that we may serve Him in return.

Most often, we associate service opportunities with being the most effective gifts we can offer, such as serving as an usher or assisting in the nursery school at church, helping to build homes for Habitat for Humanity, cooking meals in a soup kitchen, or participating in a fundraiser for the Make-A-Wish Foundation. I personally have become active in building beds for Sleep in Heavenly Peace, an organization that donates them to the surprisingly inordinate number of kids in the United States that sleep on the floor, curl up on a couch, or otherwise don't have their own bed in which to lay their head each night. Colossians 3:23 says, "Whatever you do, work at it with all your heart, as working for the Lord, not for human masters." Gifts to the Lord are most apparent in a charitable, church, or nonprofit setting, but when you apply this verse to your job and career, it can completely redefine how you view your God-given personal gifts.

For example, as a pilot, when my alarm goes off at 4:00 a.m., there are mornings I just don't want to roll out of bed. Other days, I'll be stuck flying all-night on red-eye cargo flights. I've found when I pray "Thank you, Lord, for giving me the skills to serve Your people to safely help them reach their destinations" or "Thank you for allowing me to professionally operate this cargo flight, as I recognize that we are carrying vital medicine that someone needs, perishable food to stock grocery store shelves, or important factory components to keep machines operating on which people's jobs and livelihoods depend," it completely redefines the way I look at serving the Lord.

Whatever it is you do, you can apply the same principle to your role at your workplace in order to make glorifying God your true mission: A teacher is entrusted with educating the next generation and imparting positive morals and values. Police officers and judges uphold the rule of law and order. Bankers offer loans to young couples eager to purchase their first home and start a family.

Tourism staff provide rest and relaxation to families on vacation. Barbers allow people to instill confidence in their appearance and feel their best. Zookeepers are entrusted with caring for animals that are extensions of God's own design of creation. The list goes on . . .

If you're a parent, be the best parent you can be, displaying God's glory to your children and teaching them the "path of life" as mentioned in Psalm 16:11. If you're a teenager, put the fifth commandment of honoring your parents into practice, and conduct yourself to glorify God in your studies, after school activities, and peer friendships. If you're a husband or a wife, recognize that God values your role as a spouse and that He put you in that position for a reason. Honor both God and your spouse in your familial roles. Make God look good in all that you do.

Serving others is particularly apparent when it comes to food and eating together. The family unit in one's own home could be strengthened immeasurably simply by upholding purposeful mealtimes as a priority. and I can't help but think how much greater this country could be, how crime would decrease, and values and morality increase if conjunctive mealtimes were a priority. Don't overlook the importance of breaking bread with your family, or as a means to serve others.

Over time, hospitality has changed in practice from welcoming a weary traveler (as was common in biblical times) to becoming an exclusive multimillion-dollar industry with hotels, spas, retreats, reservation-only restaurants, and private yacht clubs. Our homes have become mini compounds with security cameras, doormen, and guard dogs to keep even the most innocuous Girl Scout cookie seller at bay. It's almost unheard of to invite a stranger inside our homes, but the gospel advancement is clear in that hospitality provides a defined role in serving one another. Jesus knew the importance of hospitality, which is why He chose to meet with His disciples a final time in the form of the Last Supper. It's pretty hard to have a meal in complete silence; exchanging thoughts and ideas over a common biological need to eat opens up doorways and breaks down barriers in ways that are difficult or impossible otherwise.

In our lives, we can embrace the personal gifts that God bestows, not only in church settings but in making ethical business decisions, empowering children and young adults as mentors, managing work teams, showing hospitality to those in need, and supporting our friends and family. Corinthians 12:4 says, "There are different kinds of gifts, but the same Spirit distributes them." Let us be good stewards of these amazing, miraculous gifts given to us so that we may glorify our Heavenly Creator and continue to grow His kingdom here on Earth.

CHAPTER 13: MIRACLE OF CHANCE ENCOUNTERS

.๑๏ ๑ๅ.

*"With joy you will draw waters from
the well of salvation."* | John 17:3

Have you ever thought about coincidental chance connections that you've had in the past? Serendipitous *Casablanca* moments that link two people together that seem too good to be true. Perhaps it was a series of events that led you and your spouse together where all of the hoops aligned just right. Maybe it was a case of being at the right place at the right time—when you weren't even supposed to be at that place to begin with. Julie Andrews put it this way: "Who could have imagined that life would have taken such marvelous twists and turns or that I would often be so fortunate to be in the right place at the right time?" Albert Einstein put it another way: "Coincidence is God's way of remaining anonymous." As a single guy, I'm still searching for my future bride, but maybe I should take a lesson from this next set of biblical examples and start hanging out next to the city water tower more often . . .

In the Old Testament, there are several examples where a man goes to a foreign land, sits down by a well, meets a girl, and asks her for a drink. All produce the same happy result: chance encounters that end in a marriage. Genesis 24, Genesis 29, and Exodus 2:15-22 all recount the story of a man meeting a woman at a water well. In Genesis 24, Abraham's servant finds Rebekah as a wife for Isaac; in Genesis 29, Jacob finds his future wife, Rachel; and in Exodus 2, Moses meets his future wife, Zipporah. These are all examples of answered prayers that people of faith knew were too good to be true with no explanation other than God Himself being at work in the details. It amazes me how many prayers must be sent up to heaven around the world at any given moment, yet God always has time for them and his switchboard never gets overloaded.

Contrast these moments with the famous story of Jesus and a woman meeting at Jacob's Well, the most famous "well story" in the Bible, and a few details instantly jump out. We know from the dialogue that this chance encounter was nothing like the other three examples. Jesus was a Jew, while the woman was a Samaritan. Jesus clearly wasn't looking for a spouse, while the woman indicated she had been married five times and was currently with yet a different man, so she wasn't in the business of looking for a spouse, either. Author Jessica Brodie sums up the encounter like this: "The story of the woman at the well is a rich example of love, truth, redemption, and acceptance. And best of all, not only does Jesus spend time with her and accept her, but He wants to spend time with us and He accepts us, too. He wants us all in His holy kingdom, if only we, too, believe." Pastor Rick Warren puts it this way:

> Time is your most precious gift because you only have a set amount of it. You can make more money, but you can't make more time. When you give someone your time, you are giving them a portion of your life that you'll never get back. Your time is your life. That is why the greatest gift you can give someone is your time. It is not enough to just say relationships

are important; we must prove it by investing time in them. Words alone are worthless. "My children, our love should not be just words and talk; it must be true love, which shows itself in action." Relationships take time and effort [. . .].

Jesus met her where she was, spent time with her, demonstrated compassion toward her, and spoke the words her heart needed to hear. Jesus knew her worth and did not look down on her or cast her aside for being a woman—or a Samaritan.

Another interesting note comes from John 4:11. In the exchange between the woman and Jesus, she said, "You have nothing to draw with and the well is deep." Jacob's Well is located under the present-day Eastern Orthodox Church in Nablus, and people can go see it and even drink from the same source in which Jacob and Joseph drank and watered their flocks near the ancient city of Shechem. When reading the Bible, it's important to act as detectives and pick up on clues that it gives us. Bible Lands explorer Barry Britnell shows us an experiment performed at Jacob's Well where he drew water from the well and poured it back in. The well is likely over a hundred feet deep. The Samaritan woman referred to the well as being "deep" in John 4:11, meaning she likely had exposure to other similar water wells during her time to compare it to. How amazing is that? Not only can you visit this ancient well, but you can see for yourself how particularly "deep" it really is, as referenced in scripture.

Back at the beginning of this book, we defined a miracle as not just a singular grand act, but something that could be as subtle as a supernatural feat. That's the type of **hidden miracle** presented in the various well stories—chance encounters that are "too good to be true," that can only be orchestrated by God Himself. Romans

8:28 states that "all things work together for good to those who love God, to those who are called according to his purpose." Isaac and Rebekah, Jacob and Rachel, and Moses and Zipporah all found their spouses through acts of divine prayer that led them together.

The unnamed woman at the well was initially a skeptic, but in Jesus, she found something even greater than a spouse—her Messiah (John 4:25). Take note of the miraculous "chance" encounters in your life, and acknowledge God working through them within you.

CHAPTER 14: THE MIRACLE OF TODAY

*"'In the time of my favor I heard you, and in the
Day of salvation I helped you.'
I tell you, now is the time of God's favor, now
is the Day of salvation."* | 2 Corinthians 6:2

Are you familiar with this song?

This is the day, this is the day
that the Lord has made,
that the Lord has made;
we will rejoice,
we will rejoice
and be glad in it,
and be glad in it.

This is the day that the Lord has made;
we will rejoice and be glad in it.
This is the day,
this is the day that the Lord has made.
"This is the Day" by Les Garrett, 1967

It's a catchy little tune. Perhaps you sang it around a campfire as a kid, or maybe your own kids came home from vacation
Bible school humming the melody. I think I learned it as a teenager
in Young Life growing up in Pennsylvania. The worship leader
strummed the chords on a guitar as I gathered with about fifty other

students at the home of that week's host family, who was graciously willing to let a bunch of kids from Central York High School all cram into their basement and praise God together.

There's something empowering and special about seeing your fellow classmates all gathered around worshiping God when you're most accustomed to seeing them in the secular setting at a public school or workplace. It's a good reminder that we aren't alone in our theological studies or worship journey; there are many other Christians out there seeking a religious path and striving to grow their personal relationships with the Lord as well. I feel the same sense of comfort if I attend a family member's church in another state, or see photos of packed worship centers in other places in the world. This may be a cold, dark world, but there are other Christians all over the place throughout it. It's empowering knowing we have allies that follow a belief system the same as ourselves. Even though we don't know every Christian, we are all making a difference for Christ and are all a part of His family. It might seem like the secular world is winning the spiritual battle, but we are truly making strides in winning hearts for God. It gives me strength and determination to press on, and I offer you the same encouragement.

The song above actually comes from Psalm 118 and is a hugely positive, optimistic Bible verse. The lesson carefully crafted by God is this: one day at a time, one moment at a time. In the Lord's Prayer, God says we should pray to give us *this* day our daily bread. Not tomorrow's meal. Not the Sunday all-you-can-eat buffet after church is dismissed. But today's food. The Israelites in the desert had to collect manna each day, and they were instructed not to try and save it for the future or else it would spoil and smell and be filled with maggots. Sick! Exodus 16:35 says they had to do this daily for *forty years*. That's a lot of daily gathering. Not to mention a lot of daily trust. A lot of reliance on God, above all else, in order to meet their daily needs.

Why does God want us focused on today? So we don't dwell on and live in the past, our regrets, what we should've done differently, or wallow in the mire of defeat. Your mind will tell you there's something you did in your past that disqualifies you, but don't let it, for today is the day the Lord has made. John 16:33 says in part, "In this world you will have trouble. But take heart! I have overcome the world." Tomorrow is a new day and a new beginning, a new chance to connect with Jesus the same way Adam would take his daily walk with the Lord in the garden each morning. We can learn from the past, and we should be mindful of the future, but the **hidden miracle** here is that God gives us *today*. In the miracle of each day, we get the opportunity to pray daily, connect daily, and thank God daily. Tomorrow is never promised, so embrace today.

Just like the catchy song that many of us learned as kids, the verses of Psalm 118 remind us that *today* is the day that the Lord has made. But in the broader context, Psalm 118 is a Psalm of Thanksgiving for today. God gave us this day—let us not forget to praise and thank Him for the opportunity to live abundantly in our communities where He has us in this moment so that we can do His will and serve others to our fullest. Take it one day at a time as you keep moving forward.

CHAPTER 15: BEHIND-THE-SCENES MIRACLE

⟡

"Give me discernment that I may
understand your statutes." | Psalm 119:125

I t's a curious thought how God is constantly working behind the scenes to direct our paths, even when it's unbeknownst to us.

At one point in my life, I had been flying regional jets for about eleven years and had grown increasingly frustrated that I was unable to advance to the major airlines. Despite having all of the hours and credentials I needed, I applied to most of the large commercial airlines in the US and none would even give me the opportunity for an interview, much less a job. It was disheartening seeing a lot of my friends move on to larger jets, flying to more exotic places, making more money, and having a better quality of life while I felt like my path stayed stagnant.

Then one day, I ran across the website for a rapidly growing airline that specializes in 737 jet passenger and cargo charter transport. I was hired sight unseen, with little more than an informal phone interview followed quickly by the opportunity to start training a couple of weeks later. Their bases were mostly in the southern US, and while I wasn't excited about the prospects of moving away from my home in the Midwest, I had begun to consider moving to Miami or the Phoenix area.

About two weeks into the class, the chief pilot came in and announced that the airline had just signed a new contract with an all-inclusive vacation company, and we would be opening up a brand-new pilot base in St. Louis Missouri, of all places—my home city! Not only would I not have to relocate, but I'd be flying a 189-seat Boeing 737-800 jet, the largest and newest in the fleet. I'd be doing day trips to exotic places like Montego Bay, Puerto Vallarta, Huatulco, and Punta Cana. And, on top of that, growth at this fledgling airline was so strong that I was able to upgrade from first officer to captain in just four months, a feat completely un-heard of in any of the other major airlines I had initially applied to.

I had filed my personal flight plan for one route, so to speak. Frustrated by my perceived failure, I was stuck in a rut and thought I'd have to move out of state to further my career. But unbeknownst to me, God had a better plan. He had been working behind the scenes and had lined up the absolute perfect timing to tell me, "Sit down, I've got this." He was actively pulling the strings the whole time, and I didn't even realize it.

The story of the prophet Balaam and King Balak takes place in Numbers 22-24. It's a story of attempted greed for oneself at the expense of a nation, but one where God was very much in control the whole time, unbeknownst to the Israelites.

Balaam was a prophet who communicated with God, but his heart was not right with God, and he intentionally led Israel astray. King Balak encouraged Balaam to entice the Israelites to eat food that had been sacrificed to idols and committed sexual immoral-ity, as recalled in Revelation 2:14. Balak conspired with Balaam and asked him to basically sell out the Israelites and curse them in exchange for a financial reward from Balak, something Balaam agreed to. But Balaam noted to Balak that any curse had to come from God; Balaam did not have that kind of power himself.

It's a fascinating story that continues with Balaam and his donkey traveling down a road where an angel, visible only to Balaam's donkey, blocked the path and he could not proceed. After Balaam whipped the donkey for stopping in its tracks, God miraculously enabled the donkey to talk! Ironically, this lowly ass had more words of wisdom than God's appointed prophet. The angel then transformed and visibly manifested itself so Balaam could also physically see it, which finally knocked some sense into him after the bizarre exchange. Just like Jonah after his extended stay in the efficiency suite of a fish, Balaam repented, changed his heart, corrected his ways, and began to follow God. Thank the Lord that when we are stubborn and bull-headed, he is as patient with us as he was toward Balaam.

Later in Numbers 23:8, after redirecting his life to follow the Lord, Balaam tells the king, "How can I curse those whom God has not cursed? How can I denounce those whom the Lord has not denounced?" King Balak wanted Balaam to curse Israel, but after Balaam sought the counsel of the Lord, he could only bless Israel. Proverbs 16:9 says, "The heart of man plans his way, but the Lord establishes his steps." On that dusty road, Balaam turned a complete 180 degrees around once the angel of the Lord corrected his ways in a "road to Damascus" transformation—the same as Saul similarly would on a dirt road 2,400 years later.

The **hidden miracle** in this amazing story is that God works on behalf of our good, even when we are unaware of it. Isn't it amazing what goes on behind the scenes? Ephesians 3:20 summarizes it this way: "Now to Him who is able to do immeasurably more than all we ask or imagine, according to His power that is at work within us." Just like the Israelites who were oblivious to the entire exchange, we are totally unaware of the spiritual battles God is fighting on our behalf each day and the ways he establishes our steps with His hand of protection over us. Rabbi Jason Sobel explains God's blessings as such:

> Divine breakthrough leads to God's promise to bless us. I've experienced blessing after blessing as I've trusted God in faith. His blessing comes in many forms, and sometimes His blessing isn't what I think it should be for my good. But when I look back, I can see how God worked things out—the blessing I thought I wanted wasn't nearly as remarkable as God's blessing.

How many times have you prayed to God not only for specific things, but also for blessings unseen or unrealized as well? In my prayers, I'll often incorporate thanks for all of the blessings He bestows on me that I'm completely oblivious to and are completely ignorant and unaware of, yet I know He has taken care of these details because He loves me. Isaiah 55:9 says, "For as the heavens are higher than the earth, so are my ways higher than your ways and my thoughts than your thoughts." Israel had no idea what was going on between Balak and Balaam. God knew, though, and He held up his shield to protect the Israelites from danger and destruction.

The next time you feel inconvenienced or like your day is interrupted, or your life upended, stop and consider the sovereignty of the Lord. There is purpose in everything, and nothing is wasted. We only see immediacy and have our own ideas and plans of how our little personal "flight plans" in life are supposed to go, but God sees the grander picture as our universal air traffic controller, directing our routing on the less-turbulent courses. God is always working on our behalf, even when we don't know it, and that's a **hidden miracle** I can graciously appreciate.

CHAPTER 16: MIRACLE PROVISIONS

"Listen to my words, Lord. Consider my lament. Hear my cry for help." | Psalm 5:1-2

It has always been my experience that during our time of need, God always provides. Just after college, I was deployed overseas with the Air Force for the better part of a year as a part of Operation Enduring Freedom. I came back to the US following that military deployment and struggled for over a year to obtain my first flying job, bouncing from temp job to temp job after having moved back in with my parents. Frustrated beyond measure, I even purchased the Illinois real estate licensing test course materials to change careers and get out of flying entirely. Eventually, I was offered a position with a new regional airline in St. Louis and moved to the suburbs just north of the airport. I wasn't making much money at all, but I needed a reliable vehicle, a new computer, and my first apartment—all 555 square feet of it. Those things all took resources, and money was tight. However, in my time of need, God provided for me. Somehow, I was able to make ends meet and ensure all the bills were paid. I even had a positive balance in my checking account at the end of the month, so I'd say I was doing more than alright.

The Bible account of the Persian wise men bestowing their gifts of frankincense, gold, and myrrh on Jesus is one of the more well-known stories of the Christmas story. Matthew 2:11 says they brought these gifts in reverent worship for the Christ child. According to a commentary by John A. Broadus, the oriental custom of bestowing gifts to a superior explains that the term "treasures" typically meant "treasure chests." And since these astronomers recognized that Jesus was not simply a "superior" leader but the King of all Kings whom they had journeyed for weeks to visit, they likely didn't hand Mary and Joseph a sack of a few gold coins or a gold bar or two; it was likely a large amount of gold worth a substantial sum.

Matthew 2 notes, "You, Bethlehem, in the land of Judah, are by means least among the rulers." Just the fact that Matthew gave that statement means that a lot of people probably didn't think too highly of this town to begin with. We know Jesus' father, Joseph, worked in a blue-collar trade and was probably a low- to middle-class individual of the day. Matthew 13:55 and Mark 6:3 state that Joseph was a carpenter, but it is hypothesized that Joseph was more likely a stone mason. The Greek word "*tektōn*" translates as "builder," and since there weren't many forests in Nazareth, Joseph likely worked more with stone and clay than he did with lumber.

We know in Matthew 2 that King Herod ordered all of the baby boys two years old and younger to be murdered, so Mary and Joseph, along with Jesus, fled to Egypt. That leads us to wonder what happened to the wealth that was bestowed upon Jesus by the wise men. Some scholars speculate that Mary and Joseph used this gold to finance their flight to Egypt, and the money could have substituted for Joseph's regular work income for a period of time. This makes sense, as Joseph would have had startup costs to establish his business in the new land after their journey. The family would also need money to transition back to their homeland following Herod's death once it was safe to return.

Another curious thought, however, is if some of the money was used to support Mary following Joseph's death. The Bible doesn't say when Joseph died, but since we have an account of Mary being present at Jesus' death on the cross and Joseph is never mentioned, we are led to believe he died fairly young. Jesus wasn't exactly raking in a bunch of income during his ministry, and it would've been custom at the time for Jesus and his brothers to support his widowed mother following the death of their father. Thus, the gold wealth sustaining his mother later in life is another possibility.

It's also possible that Jesus used this wealth to finance his early education, provide the startup funds for his ministry, and later finance his travels with the disciples. Jesus often taught about money during his ministry. To give warnings about money and wealth, it's possible that many of these parables were very much personal anecdotal warnings that he experienced firsthand, having experienced the very temptations with money that we also struggle with.

At the heart of our Christian walk is the fundamental understanding of stewardship and that everything we have belongs to God. We are managers of all of God's resources, including money. Martin Luther said, "There are three conversions necessary: the conversion of the heart, the conversion of the mind, and the conversion of the purse." What will we choose to do with our own abundance?

While there is quite possibly a **hidden miracle** here, the Bible doesn't explain how much wealth the wise men brought, nor whatever became of it, so any ascertaining is purely speculative. We are merely left to ponder the different possibilities of how Jesus and his family used the wise men's wealth. In any case, let us heed Jesus' statements regarding money and our Spirit-led judgment to strive to be good stewards of the gifts He gives us and the blessings that He bestows.

CHAPTER 17: MIRACLE OF LIFE ANEW

֍֎ ֎֍

"For I consider that the sufferings of this present time are not worth comparing with the glory that is to be revealed to us." | Romans 8:18

Years ago, I was stationed in Germany as a staff sergeant and was working the night shift at the now-shuttered Rhein Main Air Base in Frankfurt. We were tasked with performing aircraft servicing in the form of delivering meals and water, emptying the garbage, driving forklifts with pallets of cargo to planes headed downrange to supply troops in Afghanistan and Iraq. Sometimes I even got to drive unique Army trucks and Jeeps and other rolling stock on and off the various cargo planes. Being away from home and everything familiar in the United States was tough, but the job itself was enjoyable and rewarding.

Well, our night shift crew worked every bit as hard as the day shift, who had more raw manpower, yet rarely got the kind of breaks and liberties the day shift did. The commander we were serving under treated the day shift a lot more favorably, perhaps because she typically worked days and was able to see that crew more often and developed a greater personal rapport with them. She almost never poked her head in to tell us hi or give us any sort of praise or thanks.

Tired of being shafted and treated like kids, I drafted an "angry email" to politely but professionally stand up for myself and my men about how we always got the short end of the stick. I sent it, but thanks to Microsoft and its beautiful un-send function, I was able to recall my message an hour later, before the commander could open it the next morning. It was a chance at redemption, an opportunity to stand down and revert back to where I was. Instead, I learned to just suck it up, keep my head down, and not make waves that could have possibly backfired and made life even more difficult for us on our deployment. Un-sending that email was a chance at a saving grace, and one of redemption for me and my enlisted troops.

The story of Joseph in the Old Testament is one of heroic redemption and forgiveness on a grander scale. Much has been written drawing similarities between Joseph's life and Jesus' parable of the Prodigal Son, but I recently discovered a fresh and unique look at the relationship in the Joseph story in Genesis that is worth noting—comparative similarities of Joseph being like us, and Joseph's father, Jacob, being akin to Jesus.

In Genesis 37, we learn that Joseph was Jacob's youngest son, and he was favored so much that Jacob made an ornate multicolored robe for him. Jacob's brothers were jealous of this, and also angered at Joseph's boastful dreams that he would one day rule over them. Joseph already had the favor of his father and had no reason to brag for attention, but because of this favoritism, we get the impression he was probably a little smug and arrogant around his siblings.

Later in Genesis, we learn about how Joseph's brothers sold him to a caravan of Ishmaelites, and through a later exchange he ended up being sold to Potiphar, Pharaoh's captain of the guard.

Genesis 39 describes how Joseph was imprisoned for being wrongly accused of attempted rape against his master's wife, causing him to spend two years in jail for a crime he didn't commit.

The meaning of Joseph's life story is this:

> The life of Joseph gives a testament of the sovereignty and grace of God for those who live faithfully and righteously. Despite being sold into slavery by his brothers, Joseph remained faithful and trusted in God to deliver him from tribulation. Additionally, this story shows how God's plan may not be obvious to our limited perspective but indeed "all things work together for good, for those who are called according to his purpose."

The comparison we can draw from this story is that like Joseph, we are all arrogant, boastful, and proud at times. We don't always humble ourselves the way we should, and as a result, our brethren often hate us for being favored, be it resentment from a sibling, a boss, or even our followers on social media. As Christians, we might even have to serve punishment and hardships because of those who conspire to do us wrong, despite being innocent and choosing the blameless path. However, the **hidden miracle** and hope found in this story is that our Father in heaven still loves us the way Jacob loved Joseph, and He always welcomes us back.

Genesis 46:29 says, "Joseph had his chariot made ready and went to Goshen to meet his father Israel (Jacob). As soon as Joseph appeared before him, he threw his arms around his father and wept for a long time." In this life, we might rise to levels of prominence and authority, but it is in our humility that we should return and meet God where He is rather than selfishly and proudly demanding He meets us where we are. Joseph remembered the father of his youth who loved him, and despite being one of the most powerful men in the world at that time, Joseph still humbled himself and made the effort to journey back home and seek out his father where he was rather than demand his father come to him.

Jacob welcomed Joseph back in the same way that the father welcomed back the son who engaged in wild living in the story of the Prodigal Son. Let us be inspired by this example of love that God is with us through all of our trials, gives us a chance at humility, and will deliver us from our Earthly hardships in the glory of His final judgment. We just have to seek Him.

CHAPTER 18: GOD'S MIRACULOUS INFLUENCE

⚘

"Get wisdom, get understanding; do not forget
my words or turn away from them." | Proverbs 4:5

There's yet another subtle miracle in the life of Joseph that requires its own chapter. In Genesis 41, Pharaoh was haunted by a vivid dream that no one in his courts could decipher, so Joseph, who was in prison at the time, was summoned to see if he could determine its meaning. Verse 16 explains that when Pharaoh asked Joseph if he could interpret his dream, Joseph said he could not but stated that God could. After God grants Joseph the wisdom of accurately interpreting the dream that details an upcoming period of severe famine, verses 39-40 go on to say that Pharaoh told Joseph, "Since God has made all this known to you, there is no one so discerning and wise as you. You shall be in charge of my palace, and all my people are to submit to your orders. Only with respect to the throne will I be greater than you."

Notice in Genesis 41:39 how Pharaoh, who worshiped polytheistic gods (little g), at last acknowledged the declaration of the one true monotheistic God of the universe—Joseph's God (big G). I've heard it said that it's easier to convert an atheist to God than an agnostic, since at least an atheist recognizes that God exists—they just choose apostasy—while an agnostic is apathetic to the whole thought of a deity and simply doesn't care. Martin Luther, father of the Protestant Reformation, says it this way: "The truth of the matter is rather as Christ says, 'He who is not with me is against me.' He does not say, 'He who is not with me is not against me either, but merely neutral.'"

Pharaoh might not have surrendered his life to the Lord in that moment with Joseph, but he did acknowledge God's authority. That's at least something; even building blocks are a start. He also specifically recognized the wisdom God bestowed on Joseph as a prophet. Luckily, for the sake of his kingdom, Pharaoh heeded the warning and enabled Joseph to take steps to prepare for the famine, and thus countless lives were saved across the kingdom.

The **hidden miracle** demonstrated by God in Joseph's life at this pivotal moment is that when we stand up for our enemies and unbelievers or submit to a higher authority, even if we disagree in principle with their beliefs or methods, people will listen and God will be glorified. We have countless chances to remain loyal to God and submit to His authority while at the same time respecting the earthly masters to whom we also yield—even if their hearts and minds aren't focused on things above such as ours. It is in these exchanges that we can magnify God with our obedience.

Consider also how there have been many instances over the years in which several individuals and teams have refused a White House invitation following their championships. In just the first two-plus years of President Donald Trump's administration, twenty major sports teams won championships, but only ten celebrated at the White House. In 2015, President Barack Obama invited the

1972 Miami Dolphins to the White House—the only undefeated team ever in the NFL at that point—but three of the players notoriously declined, citing "political differences." Albert Pujols and Tony LaRussa from the St. Louis Cardinals also refused to visit President Obama after winning the World Series. So it's not particular to either a conservative or a liberal administration.

Taking a lesson from the story of Joseph and Pharaoh, we should most definitely respect political offices of power, regardless of which party is in power. After all, Romans 13:1 says, "Let everyone be subject to the governing authorities, for there is no authority except that which God has established. The authorities that exist have been established by God." However, it's still possible to courteously venerate a political leader or the institution of government of which you dissent without sacrificing your faith and ideals. Just look how God amplified Joseph's influence as a result of his respect for higher authority—elevating him to second in power in the entire world.

The moral of the story is if you get a dinner invite from a person of authority like your governor, senator, congressman, or the president—take it. God is moving in you and through you. Think about the power and influence Christians could have if we all recognized the ascendancy of the Holy Spirit and used that guidance to orient our lives. We could exert influence and change the hearts and minds of unbelievers and those who have gone astray in our own families, workplaces, communities, or whatever platform we have access to.

I like the New King James Version translation of Matthew 5:15 that eloquently states, "Nor do they light a lamp and put it under a basket, but on a lampstand, and it gives light to all who are in the house." God wants our light to shine brightly before Him and before others. C. S. Lewis said, "It is easy to acknowledge, but almost impossible to realise for long, that we are mirrors whose brightness, if we are bright, is wholly derived from the sun that shines upon us." Casting the light of Jesus we have inside us onto others is our calling. We can stand apart in our workplaces by guarding our tongues, being hospitable toward others, respecting our bosses and supervisors, and diligently and faithfully completing our tasks "as if [. . .] serving the Lord" (Ephesians 6:7). We should consider it a priority to vote for and install strong Christian leaders in prominent positions, such as on school boards, in political offices, as heads of committees, and as corporate officers. Christian solid in their walk can have huge positive consequences in our workplace settings, government, and social organizations that can permeate our society and spread like wildfire. Wouldn't that be an amazing cultural transformation to witness?

On a related note, I'm dismayed and saddened by the number of "silent Christians," as I call them, who once regularly attended church and were active in their faith journeys only to lose their way. Sometimes it's because of a breakup with a significant other with whom they used to attend. The habit of regular assembly falls by the wayside, and they grow apart from church. I've seen other friends who struggle to navigate young adult transitions from high school to college to starting a job in a new city. While their activity and engagement in corporate worship were once high, there is a certain fear of individually taking the active steps of finding a new church home. So, instead, they become "homeless Christians" who settle for watching an infrequent online church service, and their prayer life becomes mediocre at best. I've also met young couples who get married and leave the church, not to return again until they have children of their own once they are old enough to attend Sunday school. Not until that point in their lives will they rekindle their own faith walk, leaving multiple gap years.

A Pew Research study came out this fall highlighting the abandonment of faith by adults. It predicts that if the number of Christians under thirty abandoning their faith accelerates beyond the current pace, followers of Christianity—once the dominant religion of the US—could become a minority religion by 2045. More broadly speaking, in the early 1990s more than 90% of Americans identified as Christian, but in 2020 that number had fallen to just 64%. Meanwhile, those identifying as "religiously unaffiliated" skyrocketed from 16% in 2007 to 29% in 2020. The study states that outside influences like "war, economic depression, climate crisis, changing immigration patterns or religious innovations—could reverse current religious switching trends, leading to a revival of Christianity in the United States," but that's purely hypothetical.

We need to reach people for God now, people who truly desire that union with God. New Testament scholar John Piper expresses:

> "Christ did not die to forgive sinners who go on treasuring anything above seeing and savoring God. And people who would be happy in heaven if Christ were not there, will not be there. The gospel is not a way to get people to heaven; it is a way to get people to God. It's a way of overcoming every obstacle to everlasting joy in God. If we don't want God above all things, we have not been converted by the gospel."

The urgent fear of our nation turning its back on God so quickly, in just a single generation of time, should be extremely alarming.

We desperately need to reach these "silent Christians" who have fallen by the wayside and help them reinvigorate their faith.

Almost all that I've met have expressed a desire to rekindle their faith once again; that glimmer in their hearts for God is still very much alive. A simple gesture of sharing a pertinent sermon recording with a friend and talking about a Bible subject relative to where they are in life, inviting them to sit with you in church, or asking if they'd like to come hang out at your Bible study are great ways of helping these silent Christians once again find a solid footing in their faith journey. Be vocally welcoming, be present, and engage in promoting positive, enthusiastic dialogue.

We can take a lesson from Jesus' interactions with Zacchaeus in that we don't have to launch into a long lecture about anyone's past or sins—just give someone one true encounter with Christ and plant that seed, and He has the power to transform their heart. John Calvin said, "Whatever a person may be like, we must still love them because we love God." We need to reach everyone we can in order to further God's plan and purpose here on Earth, as that's what we are called to do. And one of the untapped markets of promoting the Christian faith is those Christians whose faith journey has stalled out.

Whether assembling with our enemies, those with fundamental differences of opinion, or simply those who have gone astray in their Christian walk, let us keep in mind the power of our potential influence in the lives of everyone whom we touch, just as Joseph did. God can work through any person or situation, as evidenced all throughout the Bible. He can work miracles out of mire and muck, so keep the faith and press on, no matter what life circumstance you're in.

CHAPTER 19: MIRACLE OF THE GARDEN PROMISE

*"But God demonstrates his own love for
us in this: while we were still sinners,
Christ died for us."* | Romans 5:8

Have you ever taken something that wasn't rightfully yours, then tried to justify it? Years ago when I was in elementary school, Mom would drop us off on Wednesday nights for the kids' choir at the Lutheran church where we were members. I was in about fourth grade, and one particular evening I remember I was heading out the door of the church after choir and happened to glance in the food pantry box. Someone had put an eight-pack of bubble gum in the donation bin. Score! I figured it would be no big deal to take it since it really wasn't food. Gum doesn't count as an actual pantry donation . . . right? I'd explain to Mom that the choir teacher gave it to us for good attendance or something. And you know what? I got away with it.

But even years later, I still remembered this moment. Time has a fickle way of haunting us, and after more than two decades of this moment occasionally crossing my mind, I came to the conclusion it was the Spirit's way of calling me to action to do something about it. So, I wrote an anonymous apology note to the church, put some cash in an envelope that would cover the cost of the item I took plus more, prayed over it, and mailed it off in an unmarked envelope to that church back in Pennsylvania. More so than confessing my selfish action before the church, it was important to me to come clean with God. I didn't want any praise or reply from the church; I certainly didn't want any sort of spotlight on me for my lapse in judgment, so I purposely withheld who I was since I wanted all focus to be on my penitence.

I like to think the current pastor of that congregation worked it into a sermon some Sunday about what not to do (covet, steal, lie, be a little brat), and what our response to sin should be when we do wrong. Hopefully, it went on to aid others in a looking-glass evaluation of their ways. For an action that on the surface seemed like such a trivial thing that I could have written off as a youthful indiscretion, I'm thankful that God cared enough about me that He let this nag on my heart decades later and that I was able to repent and ask for forgiveness.

In Joshua 7, we learn the story of Achan and how he plundered from God that which wasn't his. Joshua and the Israelites had just conquered Jericho, and their next region to defeat was Ai. God had given the Israelites the promised land, and if they were careful to follow his instructions, all of the enemies standing in their way would be easily overtaken and purged from the territory. Joshua 6:9 carefully points out that in their conquest, God commanded, "All silver and gold, and every vessel of bronze and iron, are holy to the Lord; they shall go into the treasury of the Lord." None were to be pillaged for themselves.

However, in the battle of Ai, the Canaanites killed thirty-six Israeli men in what was supposed to be an easy skirmish. Joshua cried out to the Lord in anguish after the mournful defeat, and God told Joshua He had removed His hand of protection over them due to sin among the ranks. It was discovered that Achan had disobeyed both Joshua and the Lord by taking a robe, two hundred shekels of silver, and a gold bar that he had hidden in a hole under his tent (Joshua 7:21). (As a side note, Judges 17:4 also mentions exactly "two hundred shekels of silver" that was used to make an idol for Micah's house. Those shekels of silver make people do crazy things—avoid anything with two shekels [about ½ lb.] of silver!)

Along with the deaths of thirty-six loyal, abiding men that were killed during the battle, Achan and his family were all stoned to death for their disobedience to God. I used to wrestle with the story of Achan, as it was hard for me to grasp why innocent bystanders had to die because of the actions of one man. In one of his sermons, Charles Spurgeon poses the thought:

> I have often wondered that only Achan did it, but that one Aiken brought defeat upon Israel at the gates of Ai. I wonder how many Achans there are here this morning. I should feel myself very much at ease if I thought there were only one, but I'm afraid that there are many who have the accursed thing hidden with them, the love of money, or wrong ways of doing business, or unforgiving tempers, or an envious spirit towards their fellow Christians.

In another of his sermons, Spurgeon goes on to warn that Satan often starts with a spark, which is the "mother of all conflagration, and though it be a little one I can have naught to do with it." Sin often creeps up like that, where a "small" sin grows into a larger one.

As a modern-day example, a recent ABC News article describes the actions leading up to the Uvalde, Texas, school shooting in which the gunman made "over-the-top threats, especially towards female(s)," was a "sociopath," and would harass his ex-girlfriend and get into fights. Tragically, the school shooter murdered twenty-one people in May 2022. Small sins left unrestrained only grew, and they impacted others in a devastating way. We mourn the innocent lives lost, but it's important to recognize that in both Achan and the Uvalde shooter's actions, the death of innocent bystanders shows how sin has the power to become a raging inferno, taking others down like a mudslide after a forest fire that wipes out everything in its path. Quite often, actually, sin isn't just a solitary condition.

The parallels in the story of Achan are peremptory to remind us of the fall of man in Genesis. The Israelites, just like Adam, had been given a parcel of land. God gives each one a clear singular restriction that is later disobeyed. The penalty for sin, as they know, is death and losing fellowship with God (Romans 6:23). Both Adam and Achan are aware of their disobedience and initially hide, and both Achan and Adam and Eve wait until they are caught instead of first admitting their wrongdoing.

While sin and death are very much at play in this world, we should remember the Eden promise that one day a man would be born who would crush the serpent's head (Genesis 3:15), the first example of protevangelium in the Bible that extends from the very beginning of creation all the way to the final riddance of Satan in the lake of burning sulfur mentioned in Revelations 20:10. The **hidden miracle** in the story of Achan is the foreshadowing of a coming savior who would redeem all of our sins, and who offers grace to mankind.

After Achan was judged, God told Joshua, "Do not be afraid; do not be discouraged. Take the whole army with you, and go up and attack Ai. For I have delivered into your hands the king of Ai, his people, his city, and his land" (Joshua 8:1). After a momentary pause, their mission was restored and once again stretched ahead of them; the Israelite's future was still full of hope. God did not renege on his covenant of delivering the Israelites into the promised land, just like He never reneged in the prophecy of a coming savior.

As with Joshua and the Israelites, God had imposed a stern warning in the judgment of Achan. But He offered His solace to quell the fears of the other Israelites who were dismayed and dejected at the deaths of thirty-six of their brethren, and He quickly restored them. God promised if they continued in obedience, repented of sin, and turned away from idolatry, He would bless them abundantly. God forgives, and the mission to continue on to conquer Ai demonstrates that He greatly desires to be in union with his people.

Paul says in 2 Corinthians 12:9, "'My grace is sufficient for you, for my power is made perfect in weakness.' Therefore I will boast all the more gladly about my weaknesses, so that Christ's power may rest on me." Praise God that the same grace that upheld God's promise of delivering the Israelites into the promised land, even after one of their own disobeyed, is the same grace that extends its forgiveness to a snot-nosed fourth grader who swiped a pack of bubblegum and took a quarter century to come clean about his crime.

CHAPTER 20: MIRACLE OF LIFE-GIVING WATER

*“If anyone is thirsty, let him come to Me
and drink. Whoever believes in Me, as the
Scripture has said: ‘Streams of living water
will flow from within him.’”* | John 37:38

am, by nature, effervescently curious about the natural world. I love learning new facts and details about God's creation, and I get especially giddy when I discover ways in which science and religion overlap and complement each other since the secular world often paints science and faith at odds.

As a kid, I can remember one particular occasion when the local high school science teacher held an evening planetarium show for the community to showcase possible ways in which the Star of Bethlehem could be explained through science. Potential explanations included a great conjunction of planets that was scientifically proven to have happened on June 17, 2 BC, similar to the winter solstice event we experienced during Christmastime in 2020. Or it could have been a comet visible in the sky during that time. Perhaps even a supernova, a star that suddenly increases in brightness due to a catastrophic explosion. Matthew 2:9 explains that the "star they had seen when it rose went ahead of them until it stopped over the place where the child was." It leads one to wonder if the star was a different celestial event that actually moved or if, given the Earth's rotation, it simply gave off the perception of moving. In any case, the wise men's journey under the darkness of the clear desert night sky as they followed a celestial light in order to greet the "Light of the World" is powerful imagery. I bet when Jesus got older, his parents couldn't wait to tell him the story about some of his first visitors!

An article from the National Academies states that many scientists who believe in God either as a "prime mover" or "active force" in the universe have gone on record stating a lack of conflict between faith and science. Kenneth Miller, a professor of biology at Brown University and author of *Finding Darwin's God: A Scientist's Search for Common Ground Between God and Religion,* says that "creationists inevitably look for God in what science has not yet explained or in what they claim science cannot explain. Most scientists who are religious look for God in what science does understand and has explained." Francis Collins, director of the Human Genome Project and the National Human Genome Research Institute at the National Institute for Health, states, "One of the greatest strategies of our time is this impression that has been created that science and religion have to be at war." He is also credited with saying, "In my view, there is no conflict in being a rigorous scientist and a person who believes in a God who takes a personal interest in each one of us." As a world-renowned scientist, he recognized the common ground that bridged the gap between science and religion.

Other examples of science supporting Christian understanding include evidence such as the marine life fossils that were found atop Mount Everest. Confirmed by NASA, these relics offer incredible evidence that a global cataclysmic flood like the one during Noah's day truly happened. Watch Jerusalem, an analyst site that "seeks to show how current events are fulfilling the Biblically prophesied description of the prevailing state of affairs of our day," says that if the entire landmass on Earth were smoothed over, there would be enough water to cover the land 1.5 miles deep. Earth as it exists today is completely different than how the antediluvian Earth looked, though even if you take Mount Everest at its current altitude, it would still be covered by more than 22 feet of water. Fish at 29,000 feet—now that's something incredible!

Evidence in the scientific discipline of archaeology consistently supports the Bible as well. *Newsweek Magazine* details that:

> In 1961 an inscription was found bearing the name "Pilate," the earliest known reference to this figure outside of the New Testament. In 1968, a first-century home in Capernaum was identified as that of the apostle Peter. In 1990 an ossuary was found bearing the inscription—and bones—of Caiaphas, the high priest who infamously pushed for Jesus's execution. In 1993, a stele mentioning the "House of David" was discovered, yanking King David out of the realm of myth and into the historical record.

Even greater archaeological evidence supports the existence—and subsequent destruction—of the ancient city of Sodom, modern-day Tall-el-Hammam. Not only was the ancient city located exactly where the Bible described it, but a five-foot layer of soot, melted bricks, and bone fragments unlike any volcanic eruption, earthquake, or fire could have produced were found. A ceramic typologist identified a jar from 1700 BC with a glassy green glaze on one side that could have only been produced by intense heat—the technology for which would not exist for another twenty-four centuries.

The scientific process I'm most fascinated with is the mystery and science behind the hydrologic water cycle. There are thousands of rivers in the world, and it's amazing how although they dump millions of gallons of water into the oceans every day, the oceans never overflow like a bathtub or sink would. The fundamental basis for the hydrologic cycle is that water from rivers and streams flows into the ocean, the sun shines on the water and it evaporates and condenses into clouds, condensation nuclei, a fixture for vapors to form around, water returns to land from the clouds in the form of snow/rain/sleet, etc., and the rivers and streams flow back to the ocean. And around it goes again, a never-ending cycle.

Ancient understanding used to be that water predominantly came from underground springs, not from rainfall and snowmelt runoff. It wasn't until the seventeenth century that French scientists Pierre Perrault and Edme Mariotte postulated the basis for the hydrologic cycle.

The **hidden miracle** unmistakably described in the Bible is that of the hydrologic water cycle—centuries before Perrault and Mariotte discovered this amazing process, and years before modern scientists ever put a name to it. Consider these supporting verses:

- Psalm 135:7 says, "He makes clouds rise from the ends of the earth; He sends lightning with the rain and brings out the wind from His storehouses."

- Isaiah 55:10 says, "As the rain and the snow come down from heaven, and do not return to it without watering the earth and making it bud and flourish, so that it yields seed for the sower and bread for the eater."

- Jeremiah 10:13 says, "When He thunders, the waters in the heavens roar; He makes clouds rise from the ends of the earth. He sends lightning with the rain and brings out the wind from His storehouses."

- Job 36:27-29 says, "For He draws up the drops of water, they distill rain from the mist, which the clouds pour down, they drip upon man abundantly. Can anyone understand the spreading of the clouds, the thundering of His pavilion?"

Four separate books of the Bible contain wisdom describing the miraculous cycle of rain, water vapors, and clouds. The wisdom above is concisely summed up in Ecclesiastes 1:7 that proclaims, "All streams flow into the sea, yet the sea is never full. To the place the streams come from, there they return again." The Bible contains miraculous wisdom about the natural water cycle that evaded human scientific understanding for millennia, yet the knowledge was in scripture all along, right under their noses.

The Bible is not an academic textbook, but it certainly hints at many scientific truths supported by both ancient wisdom and modern-day evidence. Science and faith will never completely be in agreement this side of heaven, because God commands faith in our response to Him, even if we don't fully understand or comprehend the whys and wherefores. But our Creator, even to this day, graciously continues to reveal more and more wisdom and understanding about our planet through incredible astronomical discoveries, biological breakthroughs, archaeological evidence, hydrology, medicine, and more.

CHAPTER 21: THE MIRACLE OF LIFEBLOOD

༺ ༻

"O precious is the flow
that makes me white as snow;
no other fount I know;
nothing but the blood of Jesus."
"Nothing But the Blood of Jesus"
Robert Lowry (1876)

Have you ever had an old car that leaked oil? I still remember a few of my first cars that dripped oil worse than a radial engine on a Kansas crop duster. Dad didn't even want me to park in the driveway, and the car was relegated to living its nights out in the road underneath a streetlight. I'd have to periodically check the oil, for if I didn't, the oil light would soon come on. And if I didn't take immediate action after that, the engine would burn up and die. It didn't matter how much gas I put in the car, if the radiator fluid was topped off, or how shiny and clean it was on the outside; oil is the lifeblood of a car. Our bodies are much the same way. We can eat all the food our stomachs can handle, drink all the water we can take, live active and nutritious lives, but without blood, the life instantly drains out our bodies.

In Western medicine, the act of bloodletting dates back to fifth century Greece. Doctors would basically drain blood from the body to cure symptoms like fevers, headaches, hypertension, gout, nosebleeds, yellow fever, and smallpox, among others. The belief that bloodletting would drain disease from the body was disproven in 1628, although it would be another two hundred years before the practice would largely disappear from the medical landscape. George Washington famously underwent five bloodlettings in less than one day in an attempt to cure him from an illness—which ultimately killed him.

National Geographic reported in 2015 that the practice had come back into prominence in some areas, particularly in India, where religious mosques would draw blood from people and the gutters would "run red" from all of the blood removed from patients. Gross! Don't forget to wear your galoshes if you take an after-dinner stroll with your sweetheart. If the ancients (and even now some Eastern societies) would have recognized the wisdom from scripture all along, they would have quickly discovered that the practice of bloodletting was counterintuitive to what the Bible teaches and that they were literally draining the life out of their patients.

Leviticus 17:11 gives us the knowledge that "for the life of the flesh is in the blood, and I have given it for you on the altar to make atonement for your souls, for it is the blood that makes atonement by the life." Blood wasn't merely a metaphor for life, but life itself. God regarded the blood of an animal to be consecrated, as evidenced by the requirement for altar and temple animal sacrifices. In Exodus 12, God required the Israelites to put the blood of a lamb on their doorposts for protection as the angel of death passed by, demonstrating the power of blood—power given by Him. Human blood is even much more sacred, designated as such by the forbidding of murder and the shedding of another man's blood (Genesis 9:6).

It's no insignificant detail that in the story of Rahab, the Israelite spies instructed her to tie a "scarlet cord" in the window of her home so that she and her family would be spared (Joshua 2:18). Scarlet is the color of blood. See the connection to the scarlet lamb's blood that the Israelites smeared on their doorposts in order to protect their firstborns while in Egyptian captivity? Isaiah 1:18 would later foretell, "Though your sins are like scarlet, they shall be as white as snow; though they are red as crimson, they shall be like wool." Years later, a Savior would come who would shed his blood for the sins of all.

Rahab may not have realized it at the time, but the rope she tied in her window would have alluded to her distant relative King Solomon's writing: "Though one may be overpowered, two can defend themselves. A cord of three strands is not quickly broken." (Ecclesiastes 4:12). Rahab was initially a "single cord" of rope, living a wayward life on her own. Following the destruction of Jericho, she ended up marrying a man by the name of Salmon (Matthew 1:5). The romantic in me can't help but wonder if he was one of the spies who helped rescue and save her. The Bible doesn't say, but Rahab and Salmon became one union, with God being the third strand of their unbreakable bond. Salmon didn't see Rahab for who she was, but for who she was called to be. In the same way, Jesus sees value and worth in you and me.

It should be no surprise, then, that the symbolism that Jesus gives to wine at the Last Supper is that he said, "This cup is the new covenant in my blood, which is poured out for you" (Luke 22:20). Blood is the essence of life, and by drinking wine and connecting it to the symbolism of bread as the body, we are literally inviting Jesus inside of our bodies as we commune with him. His power is within us, sustaining us. That's the overarching theme of this **hidden miracle**—*life itself* is in the blood of every living creature and is sacred according to God.

Romans 3:25 says, "God presented Christ as a sacrifice of atonement, through the shedding of His blood—to be received by faith. He did this to demonstrate His righteousness, because in His forbearance He had left the sins committed beforehand unpunished." When Jesus came and offered up His life by pouring out His blood on the cross, the perfect sacrifice had finally been made. Hebrews 9:14 says, "How much more, then, will the blood of Christ, who through the eternal Spirit offered himself unblemished to God, cleanse our consciences from acts that lead to death, so that we may serve the living God!"

Food is the fuel that we consume—the gasoline that powers our bodies. But blood is the vital silent lubricating oil we need to run our individual bodies, as consecrated by Jesus. Life is in the blood, and miraculous eternal life is in the blood of Christ.

CHAPTER 22: THE MIRACLE OF HOME

☙ ❧

"By wisdom a house is built, and through understanding it is established." | Proverbs 24:3

When I was younger we moved around a lot, and I lived in several different houses. There were various transitions of bouncing between different schools and the adjustment of getting used to new neighborhoods. The challenges of meeting new friends was something that was hard for me, as I'm somewhat of an introvert. Despite all of the changes, though, my most important needs were always met. Life was hectic, but I always had Mom and Dad and my brother and sister with me. No matter which particular bus I got off at the end of the day from whatever school district, my black Labrador, Cody, was always there to greet me. Mom still made the same recipes and my favorite foods that I loved no matter where we were. My closet was always full of my clothes wherever we went. And our family customs and traditions never wavered despite all of the crisscrossed miles. I learned to look at home as my base camp, wherever home happened to be at that moment. While my life sometimes felt like a tetherball being punched around, the post was secured deep in concrete and it never moved. Home was a constant. I never had to worry about my needs being met.

We can read the words Jesus Himself spoke during his Sermon on the Mount and the assurances we have when we make our home with God. Matthew 6 begins with Jesus warning us against being sanctimonious in our charitable giving, avoiding the hypocrisy of praying in public just to be seen by others, the importance of humbleness and sincerity when communing with our Father, extending forgiveness to others in the same way our Father extends forgiveness to us, and warnings to resist financial temptation and greed in recognizing that man cannot serve both God and money. The chapter concludes with the challenge to avoid worry and trepidation.

Jesus had just loaded up his followers with a long sermon on "do this," and "don't do that." I'm sure anxiety and stress was running high, being weighed down with all these instructions all at once, as He was largely redefining the traditional religious teachings that the people had long been taught from an early age. It was a lot to take in, and a great challenge for His followers to live up to. But at its core, the Sermon on the Mount speaks even today to how God the Father cares more for the hearts and minds of people than their outwardly extreme adherence to rote religiosity.

Matthew 6:25-26 goes on to say:

> Therefore I tell you, do not worry about your life, what you will eat or drink; or about your body, what you will wear. Is not life more than food, and the body more than clothes? Look at the birds of the air; they do not sow or reap or store away in barns, and yet your heavenly Father feeds them. Are you not much more valuable than they?

Verses 31-32 reinforce that lesson as well: "So do not worry, saying, 'What shall we eat?' or 'What shall we drink?' or 'What shall we wear?' For the pagans run after all these things, and your heavenly Father knows that you need them." When our home is in the Lord, God takes responsibility for looking after us and taking care of us. I'll be the first to admit that it is easier said than done, but there is little worth in stressing and worrying about our safety, security, and needs when we abide in the house of the Lord.

King David knew the importance of residing in God's house. He mentioned it several times in his writings, including Psalm 26:8, "Lord, I love the house where You live, the place where Your glory dwells," and most famously in Psalm 23:6, "Surely Your goodness and love will follow me all the days of my life, and I will dwell in the house of the Lord forever." The **hidden miracle** here is that when we make our home with the Lord, we can leave the Fatherly responsibilities of providence up to Him and check our worries at the door. When we abide in the Lord, we have the freedom of knowing He will care for our needs, as our physical bodies are the home for our soul and the Holy Spirit that resides inside. When we release the energy we expend due to worry, we can refocus this anxiety into union and community with God. With that freedom comes safety, security, and lasting peace.

Furthermore, let us not think that we have too much baggage to make our home with God and thus decline his invitation. Psalm 55:22 says to "cast your cares on the Lord and he will sustain you; he will never let the righteous be shaken." We can show up to God's house pulling a U-Haul trailer full of past sins and regrets—with luggage hanging off the back, too, because we're carrying around so much—and He still welcomes us.

Remember the Parable of the Prodigal Son in Luke 15 and how excited the boy's father was to greet him? If we seek the Lord with all our hearts, confess our sins, and humble ourselves before the cross, God welcomes us with open arms. God is the greatest host ever, and there will always be a proverbial room for us, a warm meal, and a cozy fire burning in the fireplace. Matthew 11:28 offers the invitation, "Come to me, all you who are weary and burdened, and I will give you rest." God never flips on the "No Vacancy" sign; there is always room for more people to join Him in His home.

One day, our mortal lives will come to a close and we will be called from our earthly houses to our heavenly homes. John 14:1-3 says, "Do not let your hearts be troubled. You believe in God; believe also in me. My Father's house has many rooms; if that were not so, would I have told you that I am going there to prepare a place for you? And if I go and prepare a place for you, I will come back and take you to be with me that you also may be where I am." C. S. Lewis explains that this "place" that God is preparing is a result of our Savior's love for each and every one of us. As he wrote in *The Problem of Pain*, "But God will look to every soul like its first love because He is its first love. Your place in heaven will seem to be made for you and you alone, because you were made for it—made for it stitch by stitch as a glove is made for a hand."

We already have a room waiting for us in God's heavenly home that Jesus is lovingly furnishing for our arrival. The Great Host assures us of that. But let us have an equal assurance that the miracle of the Lord's hospitality in providing for our every need also extends to us here today. We just need to open the door and step inside.

CHAPTER 23: MIRACLE OF SOLITARY PRAYER

. споза.

"But you, Lord, do not be far from me.
You are my strength; come quickly
to help me." | Psalm 22:19

n your prayer life, how do you connect best with God? I'll admit that I most frequently and regularly commune with God just before bedtime, though I've long discovered this isn't my most effective prayer time. Lying prostrate in bed, exhausted from the day's activities, means my mind usually has trouble focusing and wants to drift into la-la land. Any prayer life is a step in the right direction, just like we can listen to songs on AM radio with fair broadcast quality. But what if there was a better way to connect with God? What if we could increase the quality of our communication and we could broadcast (and receive) in digital FM quality? Higher quality is always better and more effective, so consider these thoughts on ways to have a stronger prayer life.

Jesus is the model of perfection for so many activities, and it's quite apparent that He regularly prayed in corporate settings in the midst of others. The example that first jumps into my mind is when Jesus fed the crowd of five thousand with just five small barley loaves and two fish. John 6:11 says, "Jesus then took the loaves, gave thanks, and distributed to those who were seated as much as they wanted. He did the same with the fish." Another example scriptural example that comes to mind says, "Rejoice always, pray continually, give thanks in all circumstances; for this is God's will for you in Christ Jesus" (1 Thessalonians 16-18). We are called to be in a *constant* posture of prayer, regardless of where we happen to be in the midst of our day's activities.

When he wanted to communicate with his Father on a more interpersonal level, scripture records a different approach in which Jesus prayed. Consider the following three verses:

- Mark 1:35: "Very early in the morning, while it was still dark, Jesus got up, left the house and went off to a solitary place, where He prayed."

- Luke 5:16: "But Jesus often withdrew to lonely places and prayed."

- Luke 6:12: "One of those days Jesus went out to a mountain-side to pray, and spent the night praying to God."

Serious and deliberate personal prayer challenges us to step out of our earthly lives and to connect with God on a mental plateau apart from our everyday world. It forces us to avoid the distractions of "noise," whether that be in the form of music, cell phone notifications, traffic, other voices, or mental diversions. It commands that we focus our full attention on God, and that we soak up His presence by being alone in natural creation.

That's the **hidden miracle** contained within Jesus' example of detachment to a lonely place: solitary places are hard to find, hard to reach, and require us to pause with the comfort of our everyday lives. They involve deliberate decision-making, discipline, and determination in order for us to reach those places. But once we are there, it is much easier to find God, and our prayer time will be much richer for it. When we seek out remote, lonely places, we will experience focus, devotion, and stillness.

Suppose you live in a big city and it is an infrequent occurrence to be able to find a solitary place to get away to pray. Guess what—Jesus spoke to that as well. The population of Palestine in Jesus' day was at least a half a million people, so it might have been difficult to regularly travel outside city cores like Joppa and Jerusalem.

Although Christianity was just beginning to make inroads in Rome at that time, its population was estimated to be four to five million males, plus women and children. In Matthew 6:6, Jesus offers guidance for those unable to get away to a solitary place and speaks to the importance of creating personal space for prayer within your own home: "But when you pray, go into your room, close the door and pray to your Father, who is unseen. Then your Father, who sees what is done in secret, will reward you."

In *Emotionally Healthy Discipleship*, Peter Scazzero quotes directly from Mother Teresa's Biography, *Come Be My Light: The Private Writings of the "Saint of Calcutta,"* which gives this wisdom:

> We all must take the time to be silent and to contemplate,
> especially those who live in big cities like London and New
> York, where everything moves so fast. [. . .] I always begin
> my prayer in silence, for it is in the silence of the heart that
> God speaks. God is the friend of silence—we need to listen
> to God because it's not what we say but what He says to us
> and through us that matters. Prayer feeds the soul—as blood
> is to the body, prayer is to the soul—and it brings you closer

to God. It also gives you a clean and pure heart. A clean heart can see God, can speak to God, and can see the love of God in others.

Even Mother Teresa, the revered, benevolent, incredibly selfless person that she was, knew and understood the need for deliberate, quiet, unrushed prayer.

I've come across many photos online of "prayer closets" that people have set up in their homes, a comfortable dedicated place to pray, journal, read their Bible, and focus on communing with God. Many affluent people have private chapels, and there are a lot of photos of those online as well—private structures within their sprawling property dedicated to prayer and connecting with God.

My personal favorite outdoor spot during the summertime is my back deck, where I can see the trees, my hummingbird feeder, and gaze out at the lake on which I live. Another more secluded spot I enjoy is a rural state park about thirty minutes north of my home. Venturing to the state park requires deliberate time and effort, is out of range of cell service, and has lots of benches and picnic tables for spending time alone with God. In the wintertime when it's cold outside, my special spot is a comfy chair in my office apart from my desk and other distractions with a table next to it where I can set my coffee and do my devotions. C. S. Lewis states in *The Weight of Glory*, "We live, in fact, in a world starved for solitude, silence, and privacy, and therefore starved for meditation and true friendship." We need those quiet moments to connect.

Whatever your secret place might be, Jesus' retreat to solitary places to pray demonstrates the subtle miracle that if we want to excel in our prayer time with the Father, we need to make the effort to seek out or create a similar place where we can give Him our full attention. Let's challenge ourselves to pursue His example and strive to emulate His frequent way of connecting to God. In this way, we will grow ever closer to the Lord. Above all, keep praying.

CHAPTER 24: MIRACLE OF AN ETERNAL REWARD

.಄ ಞ.

"Am I now trying to win the approval of human
beings, or of God? Or am I trying to please people?
If I were still trying to please people, I would
not be a servant of Christ." | Galatians 1:10

Some people intrinsically need more affirmation in life than others, which is one of the biggest reasons why I think TikTok videos and Instagram influencers are so popular nowadays. Tattoos, crazy hairstyles, and unusual piercings are another way that people cry out for attention, and some folks just require those icebreakers and conversation starters to feel noticed or to have the spotlight cast on them. The same could be said for gear-heads who "trick out" their car with undercarriage lights, spoilers, racing stripes, and loud, obnoxious sound systems.

Other people are naturally more self-confident, self-assured, and poised in who they are, and as a result, they blend into the background. They don't dress flashy, they might be timid and quiet, and they tend to be more conservative and reserved in nature. They won't stand up in front of a church and give a heart-wrenching testimony or live in a zealous, demonstrative way.

I'm pretty introverted myself and just like to do my own thing in life. I keep to myself, and I don't seek the limelight or attention.

Plus, I think it's kind of fun to be a bit of a mysterious personality—keeps people guessing that way. Although I'm sure more than one ex-girlfriend of mine will tell you those reserved personality traits of mine drove them nuts.

More broadly speaking, one's self-promotion oftentimes mimics one's leadership style. Leaders who are self-absorbed oftentimes lead from a position of furthering one's own growth or position within an organization, and ethnocentrism within an organization can make a church or organization devoid of the ability to look outside itself to serve in the greater mission field.

To the other extreme, monasticism and asceticism are actually urged in some religious settings. Numbers 6:2-3 talks about the "Nazarite vow" during Old Testament times where during certain periods, the Israelites would abstain from cutting their hair or drinking strong drinks or wine (If you remember the story of Samson with the long hair, he was a Nazarite). Vows of celibacy, keeping vigil, meditation, and fasting on an excessive basis would also go along with the general principles of ascetic austerity. All of those practices take the focus off oneself and redirect it to concentrate on God, but Numbers 6:5-6 cautions that any sacrificial vow should only be for a "period" of time, and not an extended posture of austerity.

I remember my time in the Air National Guard when each month, near the end of drill, we would stand in formation and the flight commander would hand out ribbons and awards to us airmen for various accomplishments. Sometimes the achievements were substantial and above the call of duty and would certainly be warranted, but many times I'd be standing there thinking, *They're getting an award for that? Why are we handing out awards to peo-*

ple for simply doing their jobs?! I never particularly looked for any specific praise myself, as I viewed my paycheck and an occasional "nice job" word of encouragement from my supervisor as the only thanks needed. But later, as I began to understand how some people require that affirmation and public acknowledgment, I started to be a little more understanding as to why the military emphasized such frequent recognition.

If you're like me, there are probably countless ways in which you give back to your community, serve in your church, or love others. One way that I like to bless others each Christmas is to donate grocery money and toys for local underprivileged kids as a part of the Noel Project that a local church in Florissant, Missouri, undertakes every December. I never meet the kids or see the families, but I pray over them, drop my gifts off, and leave the rest up to God. I don't seek thanks, because I want the Glory to be to God and the focus on Him. Similarly, there's a character in the Bible who is almost but a footnote, only mentioned a few times. He received very little recognition and attention in his time, yet there is a great lesson to be learned about his life.

In addition to James, son of Zebedee, and James, the brother of Jesus, there was also James, son of Alphaeus, one of the twelve disciples who are mentioned in the New Testament as being in Jesus' inner circle. In Mark 15:40, he is referred to as "James the Less," with "less" meaning small or younger. We know very little about James, as he does not receive anywhere near as much print as John or Peter do, but we do know that James was equally handpicked by Jesus to be one of the twelve—an incredible honor. And we also know that, like the other eleven disciples, James gave up everything he had in order to follow Jesus.

The Bible reveals some overarching clues demonstrating his importance as an apostle in the afterlife. In Matthew 19:28, Jesus told the twelve, "Truly I tell you, at the renewal of all things, when the Son of Man sits on his glorious throne, you who have followed me will also sit on twelve thrones, judging the twelve tribes of Israel." We also know from Revelations 21:14 that James' name will be inscribed in the new Jerusalem: "The wall of the city had twelve foundations, and on them were the names of the twelve apostles of the Lamb." Though debated, some scholars even believe that James was the first disciple to witness the risen Lord, as mentioned in 1 Corinthians 15:7.

Although James was called "the Lesser" here on Earth, he will in no way fade into obscurity in the afterlife. History records state that "he was thrown from the walls of the Temple for refusing to renounce his faith in Christ, then stoned and clubbed to death after he fell, still praying for those who were killing him." His time on Earth was made complete in his faithful dedication to service as one of the apostles, and Jesus clearly chose him for a reason. Colossians 3:23-24 challenges us, "Whatever you do, work at it with all your heart, as working for the Lord, not for human masters, since you know that you will receive an inheritance from the Lord as a reward." Galatians 6:9 further encourages, "Let us not become weary in doing good, for at the proper time we will reap a harvest if we do not give up."

The **hidden miracle** here is that just as in the life of James, God absolutely sees you and recognizes your service and love for Him, even if you receive little press or accolades here on Earth. You may serve in your family, church, or community and receive little praise or thanks, largely leading a life of obscurity, but the challenge posed by the life of James is to dedicate our ultimate service to the Lord regardless of the acknowledgment we do or do not receive.

Whether I have one more day left in my life or fifty years ahead of me, my hope and prayer is that I have given my fullest effort to abide by the reflection written in 2 Timothy 4:7 near the end of Timothy's life: "I have fought the good fight, I have finished the race, I have kept the faith." Additionally, my ultimate goal is that I've helped lead people to Christ and have encouraged other Christians to strengthen their relationship with Jesus. I don't seek fame or honor here on Earth, because I'm confident my eternal reward awaits me in Heaven.

If you feel like a small, unsung hero, living a life of obscurity as you faithfully toil in service to God, take heart in that just like James the Lesser, you will one day meet Jesus and instantly receive the recognition you deserve. Seeing Jesus give you a smile as you walk into heaven one day as His faithful servant will be well worth all the years of thankless sacrifice and humble service.

CHAPTER 25: THE MIRACLE OF HEAVENLY WISDOM

.ಆಿ ಕ.

*"Who is wise and understanding among
you? Let them show it by their good
life, by deeds done in the humility that
comes from wisdom." | James 3:13*

I f you had all the money and all the intelligence there ever was, how would you use it? Would you use wisdom to shrewdly make business deals to gain even more money, conquer your enemies, woo love interests for physical pleasure, and be conceited and vain in every way possible just because you could? Or would you commit the extra time on your hands brought about as a result of your life of luxury to chase after Godly pursuits instead?

If I ever came into a windfall, in addition to my hopeful Bible prayer garden pursuits, I've always thought it would be exciting to start a foundation that establishes itself by supporting worthy philanthropic causes. Coupling my spiritual gifts of aircraft piloting skills with the luxury of available time, I've thought that purchasing a single-pilot jet where I could partner with local churches to fly humanitarian relief supplies in times of disasters, transporting folks on mission trips, and organizing last-minute medical relief missions would be fulfilling, unique in service to both God and man. I would retire from my day job, but not have a complete absence of work by any means; rather, I would redefine my career into a more focused kind of hands-on kingdom work.

There's a fellow in the Bible who did, in fact, have it all, but he misappropriated the blessings he was given and regretted it in the sunset years of his life.

Second only to Jonah, if I could meet any biblical personality, it would be King Solomon. I find his larger-than-life character fascinating. The son of King David, Solomon was brilliant, industrious, charismatic, and richer than Midas. He was a writer who didn't mince words, an influential leader revered even by the Queen of Sheba in Arabia. I'm intrigued by the mining operation he ran, and to this day the mystery to discover solid confirmation of the site of Solomon's copper mines that partly financed his empire continues.

Solomon is credited with being the wisest man there ever was, a gift given directly from God, but wisdom is nothing if not applied properly. Many wise people today have intelligence and IQs far superior to mine, but make some pretty dumb decisions, deny God and His commandments, and chase after folly. Like the wind of a dusty prairie, wisdom is wasted if it's not harnessed and put to good use. I might have the wisdom that I need to stop at a red light, but if I consciously decide to blow through an intersection and get hit by another vehicle, I've negated applying that wisdom and thus have to suffer the consequences. It should also be noted that misusing or denying the wisdom we've been given oftentimes has repercussions for others, too, as evidenced by the other motorist in this scenario possibly suffering an injury.

Solomon is credited with writing the book of Ecclesiastes, which is a very difficult book to read due to its depressing tone. Phrases like "'Meaningless! Meaningless!' says the teacher.

'Utterly meaningless! Everything is meaningless'" in Ecclesiastes 1:2, and repeated again in 12:8, show how later in his life Solomon severely regretted his pursuit of earthly gain. He used the phrase "under the sun" twenty-nine times to emphasize that despite applying his wisdom in pursuit of obtaining money, building projects, and physical pleasure, we only get so many trips around the sun, and someday we will all pass away. What benefits will all of our earthly procurements have for us then?

The **hidden miracle** in the overarching life of Solomon—and I believe the fundamental reason God granted Solomon so much wisdom and "earthly gain" in the first place—is to explicitly show us that none of those pursuits will help us in the afterlife. Solomon's life existed as a lesson in true wisdom expressed later in the New Testament to "seek first His kingdom and His righteousness, and all these things will be given to you as well" (Matthew 6:33). Solomon summed up his lesson for us at the very end of the chapter with his best advice of all: "Now all has been heard; here is the conclusion of the matter: Fear God and keep His commandments, for this is the duty of all mankind. For God will bring every deed into judgment, including every hidden thing, whether it is good or evil" (Ecclesiastes 12:13-14).

If even the lowliest of us subscribe to this advice early on in our lives, we will be figuratively *richer* and *wiser* than King Solomon ever was himself. Whoa . . . now that's a big thought! Solomon was spiritually bankrupt and frustratingly depleted at the end of his life, but his tale serves to impart his wisdom for us to heed his warnings.

We have an earthly responsibility to use our God-given wisdom and spiritual gifts for good, but thankfully God looks not only at our decisions and deeds but also matters of the heart. If you've made some pretty dumb decisions in your life, as I know I have, remember the wisdom that God *can* and *will* offer you forgiveness if you repent of your sins and call on His name. Solomon, in all of his wisdom, remembered that, but not until the end of his life, and thus dearly regretted his folly.

CHAPTER 26: MIRACLE OF SCRIPTURE FOR THE WIN

. oᙬ ᙬ.

"When darkness veils his lovely face
I rest on His unchanging grace
In every high and stormy gale
My anchor holds within the veil
On Christ the solid rock I stand
All other ground is sinking sand."

"On Christ the Solid Rock I Stand"

Robert Critchley (2007)

One of the toughest moments and greatest tests of my life was the summer of 2000 when I was shipped off to Air Force basic training at Lackland AFB. My time in boot camp stretched over June, July, and August, the three hottest months of the sweltering Texas summer, and the training was a test not only of my physical willpower but also my mental strength. Upon graduation in early August, I had no desire in my life to ever return to the gosh-forsaken city of San Antonio, although my tone has softened a bit since then. However, despite the challenges I faced, I recognized that I had emerged through that intensely difficult season with the knowledge I needed in order to be in top shape for any battle or obstacle that came along—a true war fighter. Drilling for battle isn't exactly fun, but the result of being in peak shape and a proactive readiness posture is much wiser than scrambling at the last minute to get spun up to where we need to be.

In Matthew 3, the Bible records Jesus' baptism by John the Baptist, and immediately following that moment, Matthew, Mark, and Luke all record that Jesus endured one of the toughest moments of his life up until that point:

- Matthew 4:1: "Then Jesus was led by the Spirit into the wilderness to be tempted by the devil."

- Mark 1:12-13: "At once the Spirit sent Him out into the wilderness, and He was in the wilderness forty days, being tempted by Satan."

- Luke 4:1-2: "Jesus, full of the Holy Spirit, left the Jordan and was led by the Spirit into the wilderness, where for forty days He was tempted by the devil [. . .]."

Wow, that escalated quickly. Jesus gets baptized, and *immediately* Satan begins shooting his flaming arrows. It's an interesting thought why a perfect Holy Spirit would lead Jesus into temptation as if misleading a young soldier right into the thick of a battle without prepping them first. After all, when demonstrating as an example of how to pray later in the Bible, Jesus says in the Lord's Prayer, "Lead us *not* into temptation, but deliver us from the evil one" Matthew 6:13 (added emphasis). When Jesus said that, I wonder if he could have been reflecting on these very moments of His trials in the wilderness.

Scripture does not reveal to us the specific details of why the Spirit would lead Jesus to be tempted. However, Colossians 2:9 tells us that Jesus was fully man in "bodily form." In order to set an example for us, I suppose He needed to demonstrate that He could endure the worst of what we endure, and this extreme temptation was a demonstration of Jesus' humanity. Charles Spurgeon explains it this way:

> Truly, the Lord Jesus might say to us who are His followers, "If I, your Master and Lord, have been tempted, you must not expect to escape temptation; for the disciple is not above his Master, nor the servant above his Lord." The fact that we are tempted ought to humble us, for it is sad evidence that there is sin still remaining in us.

So, we have some clues as to why the Spirit led Jesus to be tempted, but how do we ourselves prepare in advance for when temptation comes our way, when the devil will try and manipulate us as shrewdly as he did in the garden with Adam and Eve? Ephesians 6 says, "Put on the full armor of God, so that you can take your stand against the devil's schemes." Now is the time to make sure we are prepared for battle. Now is the moment to ensure we are ready for war—not when the devil's intercontinental ballistic missiles are already inbound and all we can do is huddle under our little particle board desk like sitting ducks and hope for the best.

The secret to prepping ourselves is found in Jesus' response to each of the devil's temptations.

- Matthew 4:4: "Jesus answered, 'It is written: "Man shall not live on bread alone, but on every word that comes from the mouth of God."'"

- Matthew 4:7: "Jesus answered him, 'It is also written: "Do not put the Lord your God to the test."'"

- Matthew 4:10: "Jesus said to him, 'Away from me, Satan! For it is written: "Worship the Lord your God, and serve Him only."'"

What we can gain from the exchange between Jesus and Satan is the demonstration of Jesus' dependence upon the word of God. Three times the devil tried to attack him, and three times Jesus responded with "It is written" and then directly quoted scripture. That's the **miracle tool** we have in our back pocket—the greatest battle weapon in our arsenal when we are spiritually vulnerable is to strike back with scripture. In each attack, Jesus didn't just ignore the temptation, as temptations typically persist and rarely go away if not confronted. Jesus didn't informally say, "Oh, Satan, why don't you just bugger off and leave me alone," do the teenager eye roll, and stick His hand up obstinately in the devil's face. Nor did He sink to the Devil's low and raise His voice and cuss him out. He went straight to the word of God, and He verbalized a firm response.

God the Father allowed Jesus to be led into temptation to demonstrate Jesus' humanity as a part of his preparation for ministry as well as an example of strength and truth in resisting sin. If we are going to renounce the devil and all of his ways, we need to know the word of God and use the power in His word to fight evil. God gives us the word; we just have to learn it and use it. Like a soldier who just won a battle, we might be weary and bruised a bit, but with each battle we win, we will be hardened with unshakable confidence to meet the next challenge from Satan when it comes our way. I don't recommend poking the bear by challenging Satan to bring on a fight, but if he does, you will be ready.

Satan thinks he's some hot-shot creature that can win the war against God, but what he doesn't realize is that his mere existence only serves to magnify the glory of Jesus Christ. God loosens His leash and Satan thinks he's got the freedom to pounce, but when we use the power of the word to combat the devil, he only embarrasses himself in a crushing loss and whimpers all the way back to his little doghouse. The schemes of the devil only serve as a proving ground for us to learn to strongly depend upon the word of God as our source of strength, truth, and a means by which we can resist sin and thus honor our Lord. God did not allow Satan to gain a foothold in this world because He was powerless to stop it but because He had a purpose for it, just as He has a purpose for you and me.

While we have assurances of eternal life in heaven, I delight in the fact that the devil's existence is liminal and his days are numbered; his ticket will soon be punched once and for all, and then Jesus will drop-kick him into oblivion—Walker Texas Ranger style.

So the next time evil or temptation befalls you, consider what scriptures you can say aloud to counteract the devil and all of his slimy, crafty ways.

CHAPTER 27: MIRACLE OF THE STUDENT TURNED TEACHER

.ಳಿ ೨ಐ.

"When we walk with the Lord in the light of His word
what a glory He sheds on our way!
While we do His good will, He abides with us still
and with all who will trust and obey."

"Trust and Obey"

John H. Sammis (1887)

Aside from Jesus, Moses is probably one of the most recognized characters in the Bible. He is famous for delivering the Israelites out of Pharaoh's Egyptian slavery camps, parting the Red Sea, receiving the Ten Commandments, and marching the Hebrew nation onward toward the promised land. But Moses didn't come from a wealthy family or a royal palace. In fact, his calling started with very humble beginnings.

In Acts 3, Moses is tending sheep for his father-in-law when an angel of the Lord appears to him in the form of a burning bush. The way the Lord interweaves details throughout scripture fascinates me, and it's truly incredible how God picks certain themes and consistently sticks with them throughout His recorded word. Not only would Moses be called by an "angel" while tending flocks, but David would later be referred to in the same way (1 Samuel 17:34). Both of these angelic appearances also point to the shepherds mentioned in Luke 2:8-11 on the night of Jesus' birth.

> And there were shepherds living out in the fields nearby,
> keeping watch over their flocks at night. An angel of the Lord
> appeared to them, and the glory of the Lord shone around
> them, and they were terrified. But the angel said to them, "Do
> not be afraid. I bring you good news that will cause great joy
> for all the people. Today in the town of David a Savior has
> been born to you; He is the Messiah, the Lord."

The shepherds of Luke 8 were the first humans who witnessed the Christ Child after his birth, and I love how God uses lowly, humble shepherds tending sheep to draw himself closer to his reverent people. As an aside, it's been speculated that the shepherds would have likely been in a particular valley next to the town that night when the angels appeared to them, causing them to physically look upward to the town of Bethlehem where Jesus was born, as if literally looking up to God above. It is possible that in each of the callings of Moses, David, and the shepherds of the New Testament, the lambs among their flock would have likely been used as sacrificial lambs in the temple, a key detail that further points to Jesus.

Moses hesitated at the mission God gave him of bringing the Israelites up out of the land of Egypt. Despite the backing of God Himself, he struggled with insecurities, the same as you and me. In Exodus 4:1 it says, "Moses answered, 'What if they do not believe me or listen to me and say, "The Lord did not appear to you"?'" In Exodus 4:10, Moses also replied to the Lord, "Pardon your servant, Lord. I have never been eloquent, neither in the past nor since You have spoken to Your servant. I am slow of speech and tongue." While it may appear that Moses was resisting God, I see it more as Moses humbly expressing his doubts. He wanted to ensure that he put on the full armor of God to guarantee all of his bases were covered with the full reassurances.

Gideon conveyed a similar sentiment as cited in Judges 6, expressing the need for reassurance. In verse 15, he questions his personal capabilities in answering the Lord's call as well, ""Pardon me, my lord," Gideon replied, "but how can I save Israel? My clan is the weakest in Manasseh, and I am the least in my family." A theme repeated throughout the Bible, we oftentimes see that God routinely chooses the weakest or the least to accomplish his greatest feats. Gideon also expressed doubts that it truly was God who was speaking to him, so he put out a fleece to see if dew would appear on the fleece while the adjacent threshing room floor remained dry. Then the next night, the opposite. In those two miraculous events, he confirmed it was in fact God sending him the instructions and not a misguided illusion of thought of his mind leading him astray.

Can you identify with that? I've had some pretty big decisions to make in my life where even though I've felt the Holy Spirit urging me in one direction, I hesitate. It's not my faith, but my confidence that is lacking. In these situations, I've prayed that *I think* I feel the Spirit moving me toward a certain path, but if I'm misunderstanding or misinterpreting what I hear, I ask God to please make it more clear so that I don't proceed in error. Absent any further word from God, I am reassured that I've fully understood His instructions.

While ultimately our obedience to God should supersede any personal doubts we have, 2 Peter 2:1 cautions us, "But there were also false prophets among the people, just as there will be false teachers among you. They will secretly introduce destructive heresies, even denying the sovereign Lord who bought them—bringing swift destruction on themselves." Listening to the voice of God commands full obedience, even if we can't see the bigger picture, but it is prudent to at least consider that we are not being led astray by sin. The devil would love nothing more than to lead us into a firestorm, one where we are inadequately prepared and inappropriately equipped. Even Mary questioned the angel that appeared to her—"How will this be [. . .]" (Luke 1:34)—to gain understanding and affirm her calling.

Moses had understandable human skepticism, too. His mission was not only to convince thousands of Israelite people of his divine appointment, but also to convince the ruthless tyrant Pharaoh to release his entire slave workforce. He was probably thinking his mission was akin to running into a burning building when everybody else is running out—*Is this really what I'm called to do?* But once we determine that the voice we hear is directly from the Holy Spirit, we need to commit ourselves to being fully invested in its message and trust His guidance.

God reassured Moses that He would be with him through the mission, and Exodus 4 tells us that God provided some specific signs to teach Moses to fully understand the power God was giving him. Exodus 4:3 speaks of Moses' staff, and when God commanded him to throw it on the ground it turned into a "snake" (NKJV literally says a "serpent"). When picked up by the tail, it once again turned back into a staff. Clever how God used this particular sign, hearkening back to Genesis when God cursed Satan to the dust as a serpent. He was literally demonstrating that with God's providence, Moses had the upper hand against Pharaoh, much more even than the serpent devil himself possessed in Eden.

God also commanded Moses in Exodus 4:6 to put his hand inside his cloak, and it turned leprous. When placed inside his cloak a second time, the leprosy was gone. When Moses voiced his apprehension because of his lack of eloquent speech, God reassured Moses that He would bless him with great articulation: "I will help you speak and will teach you what to say" (v. 12). God's instructions were a crash-course on public speaking being instilled in Moses.

The **hidden miracle** we see at this moment in Moses' life is that through divine preparation, God was teaching the student to become the teacher. The conversations between God and Moses, the instructions given by God, and the signs and wonders God told Moses to perform were all obvious outwardly divine miracles. But the more miraculous divine intervention in this moment is the internal education, knowledge, and confidence that God was ingraining in Moses to become a leader. God effectively removed Moses' insecurities, doubts, and inadequacies.

How does a lowly shepherd become the leader of a great nation, performing signs and wonders on behalf of God? How can an eighty-plus-year-old man simply lower his staff, command the the Red Sea to close, and crush Pharaoh's chariots? How does one go from student to leader? It is with the divine blessing of the Spirit of God working in our lives, and the poise and confidence He instills in us.

Moses started as a skeptic, full of doubt and apprehension, but grew in his walk of faith and learned to fully trust God. Let us learn from this great leader the miracles we can do for God when we humble ourselves as His student and fully trust and obey.

CHAPTER 28: MIRACULOUS ROBE OF RIGHTEOUSNESS

✦

*"As he went along, people spread their
cloaks on the road."* | Luke 19:36

I n the story of the Prodigal Son as recorded in Luke 15, Jesus told
the Pharisees and scribes a story of two brothers. These brothers
lived with their family and had all they needed to make them
happy, but the younger brother eventually grew restless and wanted to leave home. He asked his father for an advance share of his
inheritance, and the father obliged, so he took his money and ran;
he split town to go visit other countries. Blowing his inheritance on
women, liquor, and foolishness, he later returned home to his father, barefoot, and penniless. The father mercifully took the younger son in, but the older son was insolent that their father would be
so hospitable toward his reclusive younger brother, paralleling the
disdain, scorn, and contempt that Joseph's brothers had for him in
the Old Testament.

Upon the younger son returning home, "The father said to his
servants, 'Quick! Bring the best robe and put it on him. Put a ring
on his finger and sandals on his feet. Bring the fattened calf and
kill it. Let's have a feast and celebrate. For this son of mine was

dead and is alive again; he was lost and is found.' So they began to celebrate." Out of all of the responses that the father could have chosen, the very first action we see is that he adorned his son not with a T-shirt and some cut-off jeans, but with the *best* robe that he owned.

I picture his son in tattered rags, clothing barely covering his body as he returned home. The first thing his father did was adorn him with choice clothing, akin to wrapping him in a great big bear hug. The father's actions are in direct response to the son's confession in verse 21: "Father, I have sinned against heaven and against you. I am no longer worthy to be called your son."

The father's response likely shocks us, at least initially. It is a wonder why the father seemingly rewards the son's bad behavior. But Charles Spurgeon explains it this way:

> Have you noticed how the robe answered to his confession?
> The sentences match each other thus: "Father, I have sinned."
> "Bring forth the best robe and put it on him." Cover all his
> sins with Christ's righteousness; put away his sin by imputing
> to him the righteousness of the Lord Jesus. The robe also
> met his condition; he was in rags, therefore, "Bring forth the
> best robe and put it on him," and you shall see no more of his
> rags. It was fit that he should be thus arrayed, in token of his
> restoration. He who is re-endowed with the privileges of a
> son should not be dressed in sordid clothes, but wear raiment
> suitable to his station.

The father doesn't reward the son's bad behavior; in fact, the son's "wild living" is not even brought up at the moment. The father is just excited and overjoyed to have his son back. He had the freedom to leave, and he used that freedom to make the humble yet wise decision to return after realizing the error of his ways.

The robe the father wrapped the son in also contains noteworthy symbolism. In a practical manner, it provided clothing for the son, but in a symbolic manner it demonstrated the father's forgiveness, the covering of shame, and the love and grace he had for his younger son. In traditional Hebrew families, the older son would have received a double portion of the inheritance anyhow, so the older son had no insecurity of which to worry; however, the wayward younger son still profited from not just his inheritance but, most importantly, the father's grace.

The **hidden miracle** that we glean is that the robe mentioned in the Prodigal Son story is the robe of righteousness that the sinner gets back as a result of their repentance and forgiveness. In traditional Christian culture, oftentimes the final symbol of a baptismal ceremony is the white baptismal robe or garment. Perhaps you have yours or a parent/grandparent's hanging in a framed case somewhere in your home. It serves as a visual reminder and amulet of the new holiness of a child becoming a child of God. It contributes to our understanding that the power of baptism has to transform us, reminding us of our rebirth in Christ.

Where else do we see the importance of a robe in the Bible? In Esther 5:1, we learn "on the third day, Esther put on her royal attire and stood in the inner court of the palace across from the king's quarters." Esther's robe gave her confidence to approach the king. Isaiah 61:10 also says, "I delight greatly in the LORD; my soul rejoices in my God. For He has clothed me with garments of salvation and arrayed me in a robe of His righteousness, as a bridegroom adorns his head like a priest, and as a bride adorns herself with her jewels." These two additional Old Testament examples of holy robes point to what we later learn in the New Testament:

"The soldiers twisted together a crown of thorns and put it on His head. They clothed Him in a purple robe" (John 19:2). While the Prodigal Son received a robe of adornment, Jesus received a robe of humiliation, mocking his power and honor as a true king.

As a covering for their shame, Adam and Eve sewed together fig leaves to hide their nakedness after the fall in the garden (Genesis 3:7). Adam's sin caused divisions in humanity similar to the divisions between the younger and older brothers in the Prodigal Son parable—both Adam's sin and the younger brother's sin pulled the family apart. But Jesus is reuniting His followers in unity once again as the Savior to all believers. Jesus was scorned and clothed with a fake robe during his kangaroo court trial, but in heaven he is rabbi to all, his ethereal white robe of royalty once again adorning him as King.

Let us then clothe ourselves in robes of righteousness as protection from the elements and a shield from Satan's arrows. But most importantly, let us nestle into the comfort and warmth of the Savior's love as we humbly repent and return to Him.

CHAPTER 29: MIRACLES CONCEALED

"It is the glory of God to conceal a matter; to search out a matter is the glory of kings." | Proverbs 25:2

As I write today, on September 11, I'm reminded of the tragic events that took place on this very day twenty-one years ago. Facing intense anguish and grief, our faith is always tested, and we are rarely ever left unchanged when a major disaster strikes. Almost always, we are either drawn closer to God or pushed away from Him. The terrorist events of 9/11 had that same effect on people. Interestingly, during the weekend after the attacks, church attendance was only up a slight six percent but has steadily been in decline ever since.

When tragedy strikes, it's easy to ask, "Where is God in all this?" but the simple answer is that He is where He's always been—in heaven, and in total control. We ask, "Why did this have to happen?" which is a much more difficult question to answer, but the short answer is that God isn't responsible for the evil acts of men today any more than He was in Biblical times. The abhorrent actions leading up to and resulting in the crucifixion of His own

Son are a testament to that. Our earthly minds can't comprehend an answer to a complex question that incorporates so many intricate details on a universal scale, but we can see the building blocks in small pieces within the aftermath of these tragedies.

For instance, despite the terrorist attacks on 9/11, we saw a reflection of our Savior's love in the hearts of Canadians in Gander, Newfoundland, who opened up their schools, gymnasiums, and their homes to accommodate seven thousand passengers whose flights were suddenly diverted to their airport. When the United States closed its airspace that morning, thirty-eight wide body jets bound for the US had nowhere else to go. The local residents of Gander baked food for stranded passengers, donated clothes, offered mattresses and sleeping bags, and even kept their Walmart store open around the clock so that passengers could obtain toiletries, clothing, and much-needed supplies.

Fred Rogers explained optimism and love as such: "When I was a boy and I would see scary things in the news, my mother would say to me, 'Look for the helpers. You will always find people who are helping.'" The hospitality of the local residents of Gander was even made into a story portrayed in a Broadway musical highlighting the massive community support that sprang into action. It's a shining example of how God's love radiates through people despite tragedy and turmoil. God has His purposes, even if we don't understand or comprehend them. As Isaiah 55:9 says, "As the heavens are higher than the earth, so are my ways higher than your ways and my thoughts than your thoughts."

As another example, take the story of the only survivor of the 9/11 impact zone on the South Tower, a man who clung to his desk to keep from being sucked out of the gaping hole left in the side of the building. Stanley Praimnath survived not only 9/11 but also the 1993 WTC bombing eight years earlier, and since then he has dedicated his life to becoming a Pentecostal pastor. Would that have happened absent the terrorist tragedy? Probably not. Just think of the thousands of people he has had an influence on since then. He credits a particular Bible verse he turned to when he opened his Bible during his hospital recovery for having such a profound impact on the way his outlook on life was redefined. From Psalm 91:1-7:

> Whoever dwells in the shelter of the Most High will rest in the shadow of the Almighty. I will say of the Lord, "He is my refuge and my fortress, my God, in whom I trust." Surely He will save you from the fowler's snare and from the deadly pestilence. He will cover you with his feathers, and under His wings you will find refuge; His faithfulness will be your shield and rampart. You will not fear the terror of night, nor the arrow that flies by day, nor the pestilence that stalks in the darkness, nor the plague that destroys at midday. A thousand may fall at your side, ten thousand at your right hand, but it will not come near you.

Life will always contain tragedies on both large and small scales so long as sin is present. It is the one reason that we should always be prepared, just as 1 Thessalonians 5:2 warns: "For you know very well that the day of the Lord will come like a thief in the night." So long as the Earth persists, God is actively involved in its daily events. Take heart that as long as you are repentant and a saved child of His, you need not fear the afterlife—whether death should come from a grand terrorist attack or peacefully in your sleep.

The story of Queen Esther, found in the Old Testament, contains a dramatic chain of events and is a Biblical lesson on how God is actively at work in our lives despite evil abounding. In this story, we meet a young queen named Esther who is summoned to King Artaxerxes following the king's banishment of Vashti, the outgoing queen, for refusing to obey the king's commands. Esther finds favor in the sight of the king for her beauty and her courage, but she initially conceals the fact that she is Jewish. In a separate setting, Esther's Uncle Mordecai refuses to bow to the king's adviser, Haman, and Haman becomes enraged and seeks to have all of the Jewish people killed. Queen Esther knows that if she reveals that she is Jewish to the king, she might be able to stop Haman's evil plot. So, she throws two dinner parties and invites both her husband, King Artaxerxes, and Haman, and she works up the courage to tell the king of Haman's plan. The king becomes enraged, and instead of supporting Haman's intent to have all of the Jews killed, the king instead has Haman impaled.

The most famous statement from this story is when Mordecai tells Esther, "For if you keep silent at this time, relief and deliverance will rise for the Jews from another place, but you and your father's house will perish. And who knows whether you have not come to the kingdom for such a time as this?" (Esther 4:14) Mordecai's speech is a testament that Esther was put in her position by God to do something to help her people, but God's plans would not be derailed either way. Now was her time to shine, but if she failed to act, God's favor would be on someone else to step up and intervene instead. She risked her life by approaching the king and suggesting the two banquets be thrown, and even more so risked her life by revealing her Jewish identity. But even so, God was always with her. Like Billy Graham said once, "The will of God will not take us where the grace of God cannot sustain us." If we stand with God and his plans, no evil person or scheme can thwart his intent.

To honor the self-sacrifice and bravery that Esther exhibited by courageously standing up to save her people from calamity, the festival of Purim is celebrated to this day by some Christians and many traditional Jews. While many Jewish holidays have strict rules and guidelines, Purim is celebrated more like a party and is described as "a little bit of Mardi Gras, Easter, and Halloween all rolled into one" with food, costumes, and a carnival atmosphere. It's celebrated in the springtime after a long dark winter and is marked by a reading of the story of Esther, the giving of gifts to the poor, and a large festive meal.

God's name is absent in the book of Esther, concealed to the eyes and ears, yet His spirit is present all throughout the story. The **hidden miracle** in the story of Esther is that God is continuously active in our lives, managing all the minute details and actively responding to us. We oftentimes think God is distant, living up in the heavens, and assume He is too busy to be bothered with our mortal affairs trying to thwart evil down here. But God's divine purpose will always be achieved, and in the story of Esther it was fulfilled even through a complex chain of events. Happenstance and dumb luck have no function in the world when it's ultimately God's hand that is active and dynamically orchestrating our lives.

CHAPTER 30: MIRACLES THAT POINT TOWARD JESUS

.ෙ෧ ෨෧.

"Whoever pursues righteousness
and love receives life, prosperity
and honor." | Proverbs 21:21

For the last chapter of this book, I decided to tackle the complex lives of Abraham, his wife, Sarah, and their son, Isaac. There is much to unpack as we dig into this family and many subtle miracles in their lives that point to one overarching greatest miracle. I purposely put it off until the end of the book, intimidated by the challenge of attempting to effectively draw the multitude of connections between the Father of Israel's life as a foreshadowing of Jesus. It was by far the most difficult chapter to write, given a wealth of information and associations pointing toward Jesus, but I'll share a bit of what I've learned over the years.

In Matthew 1, we learn the genealogy of Jesus, and in it we can see that Abraham lived twenty generations after Adam and ten generations after Noah. There were then fourteen generations from Abraham to David, another fourteen from David to the Babylonian captivity, and then fourteen more from the exile to Christ, so as to give a contextual timeline of where Abraham fit into Biblical chronology.

Faithfully trust, obediently follow. Those words could be a summary of so many heroes in the Bible, but none more so than Abraham. Abraham (then called Abram before the Lord later gave him a new name) came from an upbringing where his father did not worship the Lord. Joshua 24:2 tells us, "This is what the Lord, the God of Israel, says: 'Long ago your ancestors, including Terah the father of Abraham and Nahor, lived beyond the Euphrates River and worshiped other gods.'" Sadly, when sin encapsulates a family and children are brought up in a corrupt environment, allegiances to idols and false gods oftentimes sideline truth. It's tough to break that chain we see even in modern-day socioeconomic or religious settings. But amazingly, and with God's help, Abraham rose above this struggle and committed his life to the one true God.

Abraham was no young man at the time, and Genesis 12 tells us that he was seventy-five years old when God called him to leave his homeland and everything and everyone he knew, which added an additional layer of tension to the situation since Abraham would have been well-established with deep roots in his homeland. But God called nevertheless, just as Jesus called His disciples to follow Him, and the calling was answered with obedience.

It's also important to note that God doesn't apply "ageism" when calling those he chooses. Joshua, for instance, was nearly eighty when he took over Moses' leadership role of leading an entire nation. Elizabeth was blessed with a child in her old age. On the other end of the spectrum, Mary, the young mother of Jesus, was but a teenager when she gave birth. David was probably only in his mid-teens when he killed Goliath. Age is but a number, one that is largely unimportant to God in His grander plan.

After a period of trekking across the desert at God's command,

God instructed Abraham to stop. It's an amazing feat that Abraham had the courage to leave his homeland, including his father, and had the wisdom to recognize and discern that Terah's idol worship was not the destructive path he wanted to choose for himself and his wife, Sarah. Abraham's zeal for God should serve as an example for all of us that if we find ourselves in unhealthy environments, we need to get out. Even if our roots run deep and we have little more than just our tent and not much else to go on, we always have God. The Pilgrims that came to America on November 11, 1620, did that very thing. They saw vast corruption within the Church of England, and after a sixty-six-day sail aboard the *Mayflower*, they landed at a place they called Plymouth in order to establish a new community where they could freely worship.

Abraham's first act upon reaching his new homeland was to establish an altar, signaling that he was "all in." He didn't simply roam the desert like a nomad, mildly curious about God and lukewarm in his commitment. He went exactly to where the Lord told him to go, stopped when he was ordered to stop, and offered worship before any further activity or settlement. And he repeated the same act of worship in establishing a second altar when God called him to move to the Hebron Valley later in his life, as told in Genesis 13:18.

The lesson to be learned is that when the Holy Spirit calls us to move in whatever way He instructs, let us follow Abraham's example to stop and pray in that very moment. Abraham's rock was not his mobile tent on wheels—his little Jayco pop-up camper with his Coleman stove. His rock was a literal stone altar to the Lord. We might not see or envision what our future will be going forward, but we can always offer thanks to God for walking alongside us and guiding us on our journey.

Abraham was credited with being a righteous man, which is repeated numerous times in the Bible (Genesis 15:6, James 2:23, Romans 4:3, Romans 4:24, Galatians 3:6). But Abraham had his character flaws as well, and there are lessons to be learned even in those moments. His faltering and struggles included lying about Sarah (then called Sarai) being his wife and passing her off as his sister during a period when he was in Egypt. Abraham and Sarah grew impatient waiting for the Lord to bless them with a son, so with his wife's urging, Abraham slept with his slave girl, Hagar, to produce an offspring. He then later deported this slave girl and their mixed-blood son, Ishmael, into the desert, where they were famished without water and near certain death until God rescued them. As an aside, it's important to remember that God sees us and is with us, even if our lowly circumstances and placements are a result of others, as was the case for Hagar and Ishmael.

Despite this faltering, the number of times Abraham is credited with being "righteous," even thousands of years later, should be a testament to the fact that God forgives. All sin grieves the Holy Spirit (Ephesians 4:30), but Abraham's life should give us hope to persevere and return to God even when we sin and screw up. God blessed Abraham as the father of a nation, so despite Abraham's blunders along his life's journey, God demonstrated that he had great overall confidence in Abraham. As 2 Timothy 2:13 says, "If we are faithless, he remains faithful, for he cannot disown himself." Abraham and Sarah might have taken it upon themselves to alter the path God laid out for them, but God's plans, as we have seen several times, always prevail.

The lesson to us in Abraham's stumbles is that despite our many shortcomings, our ultimate obedience will yield God's full confidence in us, too. My hope is that each and every one of us will be credited as being a righteous follower, faithfully carrying out His will for us here on Earth.

After Abraham reached Hebron, he lamented to God that he and Sarah still had no offspring to carry the family forward. God assured him in a promise that the blessing of a male child was sure to come. It should not be lost on us that Abraham and Sarah's struggle with infertility, and later Isaac and Rebekah's same struggle, underscores the fact that the promised Messiah could not have been born without God's miraculous intervention in the fertility cycle—the same divine intervention that God performed when Mary became laden with the very child who would become our Savior. God has a way of weaving little clues into scripture that point to supernatural events that come to fruition later in history. By displaying obscure details like this, God demonstrates that He transcends generations and millennia, and we see numerous times that His promise of a Messiah was reaffirmed all throughout Old Testament history.

God blessed Abraham and Sarah with a son, Isaac, and Abraham is tested by the Lord a few years later in Genesis 22:2 when God says, "Take your son, your only son, whom you love—Isaac—and go to the region of Moriah. Sacrifice him there as a burnt offering on a mountain I will show you." This sounds rather similar to how Jesus was also tested in the wilderness.

Abraham's testing by God is specifically referenced in John 3:16, probably the most well-known verse of all time by Christians and non-Christians alike: "For God so loved the world that He gave his *one and only Son,* that whoever believes in Him shall not perish but have eternal life." Abraham is referred to as the "father," paralleling God our Father, and Isaac was Abraham's "one and only son" who was to be the Passover Lamb that day, just like Jesus was God the Father's one and only son. But at the last moment, God intervened and commanded Abraham to spare Isaac's life, instead providing a nearby ram whose horns were caught in the thicket to be sacrificed instead (a ram being an adult male lamb). The test of Abraham points to all of us who are bound for death, but thankfully Jesus would be our Lamb who would be sacrificed in place of our sins for our redemption.

It would be an understatement to say that Isaac's mental anguish was likely overwhelming in the harrowing moments when they walked up Mount Moriah, in much the same way Jesus's mental anguish was excruciating as He carried his cross to Golgotha along the Via Dolorosa. Both knew that their father was leading them to be sacrificed, yet still they willingly cooperated with God's plan. Isaiah 53:7 tells us, "He was oppressed and afflicted, yet he did not open his mouth; he was led like a lamb to the slaughter, and as a sheep before its shearers is silent, so he did not open his mouth." When Isaiah spoke this, he was recalling Abraham and Isaac's story but at the same time prophesying Jesus and His heavenly Father's account yet to come. Both Jesus and Isaac were cooperative in doing the will of the Father, demonstrating obedience unto death.

Genesis 22:3 contains an unusual but important detail that would also point to the future Messiah, in that Abraham "saddled his donkey" to head up to Mount Moriah to offer Isaac as a sacrifice. Horses were the method of swift transportation for warriors and nobility, but donkeys were the slow mode of transportation typically owned by the poor, the lowly, and the common man. Abraham wasn't the only righteous person in scripture who saddled their donkey when summoned by God, and we learn in Exodus 4:20 that

"Moses took his wife and sons, put them on a donkey and started back to Egypt," divinely appointed by God to further the mission of advancing the nation of Israel.

In yet another story, 1 Kings 13 references an unnamed prophet "riding a donkey" who was killed and martyred for his faith. All of these verses allude to the New Testament Savior, Jesus, who would ride a donkey into Jerusalem on what we now refer to as Palm Sunday to fulfill the divine mission of sacrificing his life for our redemption.

The progression leading up to the point where God spared Isaac's life is filled with other literary foreshadowing that points to the coming Messiah as well. Genesis 22:6 says, "Abraham took the wood for the burnt offering and placed it on his son Isaac" in much the same way that Jesus was forced to carry the wood for his sacrifice in the form of a wooden cross. Rabbi Jason Sobel points out:

> Isaac asked his father about what they would offer as the sacrifice (Genesis 22:7). He understood that he was going to be slaughtered but continued voluntarily, completely submissive to the will of his father. This foreshadowed Jesus, who asked the Father three times to please take the cup from Him but in the end submitted by saying, "Yet not My will, but Yours be done." (Luke 22:42)

Both Isaac and Jesus were willing to submit up to the point of death if it pleased God and fulfilled His will. Isaac was bound to the wood to be sacrificed in Genesis 22:9, similarly to how Jesus was bound to the cross, both literally and figuratively, and was "pierced for our transgressions" as prophesied in Isaiah 53:5.

Genesis 22:4 makes the important distinction of mentioning

the "third day" as the specific day of the week that Abraham was tested by God. The elements found in Jesus' sacrificial death and burial are also found in Genesis 1:9-11. We learn that God created trees and formed the land on the "third day," the tree being the wooden cross structure that Jesus was crucified on, and land/earth as the dust from which we were all made from with God's creation of Adam from clay, and to which we will all return again, absent Jesus' return first (1 Corinthians 15:21). Hebrews 11:19 says that "Abraham reasoned that God could even raise the dead, and so in a manner of speaking he did receive Isaac back from death." We know from scripture that Jesus was raised from the dead on the "third day" according to 1 Corinthians 15:4. Rabbi Jason Sobel says, "This points to Jesus, who performed His first miracle of turning water into wine on the third day, was crucified at the third hour, experienced three hours of darkness on the cross, and rose on the third day in fulfillment of prophecy."

It's also an imposing thought when speaking of God's creation of land and trees on the "third day" that we cannot overlook the power that those two elements have. Soil and land have the life-giving power within them to grow grand trees. In Genesis, we learn of the Tree of Life (Genesis 3:22) and the Tree of the Knowledge of Good and Evil (Genesis 2:17), both created on the third day. We know little about the dichotomy and structure of each of these mysterious trees, but we do know that each tree was vital for sustaining life in the original plan God had ordained. Trees are good in that they provide shade, a place of rest, and life to all kinds of creatures—but we also know that trees have the power to bring sin into the world, as evidenced by the tree in which Judas took his life and hanged himself on, and the death tree that Jesus carried to

Golgotha in the form of a wooden cross.

Soil and earth provide life-giving nutrients to trees and all sorts of other plants, and land serves as an anchor for trees to hold fast to as they weather storms. God divinely created man out of dust, "then the Lord God formed a man from the dust of the ground and breathed into His nostrils the breath of life, and the man became a living being" (Genesis 2:7). But earth is also rubbish, loam, and dirt; it's composed of decaying matter, compost, and ash. For those reasons, God forced Satan to eat dust when he cursed him in the garden after the fall (Genesis 3:14).

The familiar phrase "Ashes to ashes, dust to dust" started as a popular religious rite spoken at funerals in past centuries. Although not exactly biblical and largely omitted from modern funeral services, it traces its roots to *The Book of Common Prayer* published in 1549 and paraphrases Genesis 3:19 when God told Adam after the fall, "By the sweat of your brow you will eat your bread, until you return to the ground—because out of it were you taken. For dust you are, and to dust you shall return."

Earth and trees have the incredible potential for promoting life, but we all deserve to "eat dust," just as Satan was relegated to, since we are all sinful beings. We will all return to dust when we are laid in a grave someday. But Revelation 22:2 gives us the hope that we will someday soon see the "trees of life" in the second coming—two trees, one on each side of the river as they yield their fruit and provide life-sustaining leaves for the "healing of the nations."

Abraham recognized that his ultimate reward was with God. His posture in life was always to position himself not for great wealth or fame, but to focus on his relationship with God and his heavenly future. Genesis 23:9 says that Abraham purchased a place called Machpelah Cave in which to lay Sarah's body. As great as Abraham was, known as the Father of Israel, the only piece of land he owned his entire life was a burial plot for him and his wife. And even that sad, small, singular piece of property was in the middle of a foreign territory, ruled by the Hittites.

We see that Abraham realized he was but a solemn, lonely stranger in a foreign world, never fully settling on Earth. He had no personal roots here to sink into, no earth to hold fast to for his home since he moved around often, as he understood that his true foundation was with the Lord above. As Billy Graham put it, "When we come to the end of ourselves, we come to the beginning of God."

While Abraham and his family had a mission and a purpose from God to fulfill, the numerous **hidden miracles** in this chapter intertwined throughout their lives all highlight subtle clues that ultimately point to the coming Messiah. Jesus is foreshadowed on many different levels throughout the life of Abraham, as found throughout scripture. We also see that Abraham's life was not free from sin and shortcomings, although he came through for God at the critical junctures of his life and followed God in both purpose and action. Abraham did not live a life of luxury in a palace; rather, he moved around frequently and resided in a tent, showing us that God never promises an easy life, but He does promise to give us all that we need. Abraham walked by faith, and in doing so was blessed immeasurably.

The little miracles and interwoven elements of scripture that point to Jesus throughout Abraham's life are small miracles that we all profit from when we accept Jesus as our Messiah.

EPILOGUE

.ରେ ୨ର.

A s we come to the end of our discovery of some of the subtle **hidden miracles** and less apparent wisdom found tucked into the Bible, I hope that it empowers you to carefully read and investigatively study your Bible with a whole new focus on how engaged with humanity God truly is. God loves you and wants to pursue a relationship with you, just as He did in all of these biblical examples, to ensure fulfillment in your life. Hebrews 13:5 says, "Never will I leave you, never will I forsake you." God's super-power is empathy. His greatest miracle is that He is with us in this moment, and He will never leave us. We have all seen friendships break and relationships end. Humans will abandon us, discard us, and cast us aside, and life seems to march on even if we are feeling lost or consumed by it. But through all of it, God is our constant.

It's crucial to seek God in prayer. 1 Thessalonians 5 16-18 instructs us to "rejoice always, pray continually, give thanks in all circumstances; for this is God's will for you in Christ Jesus." Along with that, I'd encourage you to disconnect once in a while and spend time alone to soak up his presence. Pray and ask. Talk to God. But leave plenty of time for silence and listening as well. Above all, trust the Lord and hold on to your eternal hope. Romans 10:9 says, "If you declare with your mouth, 'Jesus is Lord,' and believe in your heart that God raised Him from the dead, you will be saved." Dedicate yourself to the cause of Christ and faithfully serve in kingdom work.

In closing, I'd like to leave you with this prayer. Thanks be to God!

.ᴑℓ℘ℊᴑ.

Dear Lord, we have studied Your works. We know of Your great miracles, Your subtle and less apparent miracles, and Your divine intervention where all the pieces fall into place in a way that could only be authored by You. We know that You know us, but now we pray we know Jesus through You. We know that You are here with us because You are not just God of the universe, but God of our hearts. David said in Psalm 46, "Be still and know that you are God." Help us to seek You in prayer and listening. Let us sense Your presence in our lives. Lead us and guide us in Your way everlasting.

Amen.

APPENDIX: INSPIRATIONAL POETRY

_⋅ഐ ഉ⋅_

"But ask the animals, and they will teach you,
or the birds in the sky, and they will tell you;
or speak to the earth, and it will teach you,
or let the fish in the sea inform you.
Which of all these does not know
that the hand of the Lord has done this?
In his hand is the life of every creature
and the breath of all mankind." | Job 12:7-10

_⋅ഐ ഉ⋅_

Lord, I Long to Feel Your Presence

Lord, I long to feel Your presence, as I search the Earth and sky
Are You with me at this moment, can You hear my prayerful cry?
As I walk with You each morning, beams of radiant light appear
Casting iridescent beauty, as You fill my heart with cheer.

In Your peace that comes with misty, morning meadows in the shade
Birds with sweet melodious singing, to my ears do serenade
Babbling brooks, cerulean rivers, with their water sparkling blue
Offer life to every creature, daily providence anew.

As the wheat fields bend with golden, stalks a plenty every year
Gentle breezes help remind me, that my Savior's love is near
See the Earth and all its glory, and the waves as they rush by
In His hand is every creature, to their needs he does supply.

Lord, I lift Your name on high
You created Earth and sky
You sustain and you provide
Only you can satisfy!

I am overcome with feeling, God's sweet company each morn
Hope restored and spirits lifted, each new daytime being born
In this walk I sense His presence, and His never-ending love
Thank You for Your grace and mercy, given from thy hand above.

"Out of the depths I cry to you, Lord;
Lord hear my voice." | Psalm 130:1-2

Little Church on the Ridge

When life is getting heavy
With burdens laden down
And troubles are surmounting
With pressures all around.
There's one who will always listen
You can take your worries to
Go up yonder, cross the bridge
To the little church on the ridge.

There's a place you can kneel and pray
To the Lord who will overcome
'neath the cedar boughs that sway
And the glistening morning sun.
As you lift your voice to sing
And steeple bells start to ring
Go up yonder, cross the bridge
To the little church on the ridge.

The preacher speaks of hope
That's found in God's own son
If you feel you cannot cope
Remember the battle's long been won.
Just keep your eyes on Jesus
And the promise that He brings
Go up yonder, cross the bridge
To the little church on the ridge.

Now that I'm old and gray
I remember beautiful days of old
Soon I'll climb the heavenly stairway
Into a celestial realm of gold
I feel the comfort, warmth, and love.
Singing praise to the Lord above
Go up yonder, cross the bridge
To the little church on the ridge.

"Stand at the crossroads and look; ask for the
ancient paths, ask where the good way is,
and walk in it, and you will find rest
for your souls." | Jeremiah 6:16

Help Me with These Things

Standing at the crossroads
Of one of life's great tests
Ask where the good path is
Where your soul can safely rest.

The Lord will grant you guidance
When it's wisdom you pray for.

Father, help me with these things
That tug at my heartstrings.

Moses prayed for Israel's rescue
As if talking with a friend
In the form of a burning bush
Pharaoh's downfall did portend.

David walked into the valley
With a giant bearing down
But with a stone and heavenly precision
Brought Goliath to the ground.

Elijah faced oppression
And discouragement all around
But after hiding in a cave
God's whisper helped his faith rebound.

The Lord will grant you guidance
When it's wisdom you pray for.
Father, help me with these things
That tug at my heartstrings.

Without wisdom from above
The path sometimes seems concealed
But with prayer to God above
His way will be revealed.

The Lord will grant you guidance
When it's wisdom you pray for.
Father, help me with these things
That tug at my heartstrings.

ABOUT THE AUTHOR

"My heart is stirred by a noble theme as I recite
my verses for the King;
my tongue is the pen of a skillful
writer." | Psalm 45:1

Brent Furrow is a Boeing 737 charter airline pilot from Holiday Shores, Illinois, who has been to all fifty states and dozens of countries around the world. He is an Air Force veteran of Operation Enduring Freedom, an Eagle Scout, and holds a BA in speech communication from Eastern Illinois University as well as an MS in recreation, sport, and tourism from the University of Illinois. His interests run deep; when he's not working, he enjoys outdoor activities like boating, fishing, hiking, learning about US history, volunteering, and skiing the Rockies. He grew up Lutheran and is a lifelong conservative Christian committed to his faith and serving the Lord.

www.ingramcontent.com/pod-product-compliance
Lightning Source LLC
Chambersburg PA
CBHW060433090426
42733CB00011B/2250